Preface:

I could call this book Teacher911, or Help for Teachers, or Teaching: A Survival Manual.

If you are thinking about a career in Education.......

If you are in the middle of a Teacher Training Program.......

If you are Certified to Teach at last and perhaps in debt.......

If you are hired and starting your career.....

If you have a few years of Teaching under your belt or you are Mid-Career...

You need to read this book!

When I retired after 30 plus years as a teacher and school principal, I kept thinking about what you really need to know for survival and success. As a school principal, I always made the effort to hire the newbies and gave them a chance, especially if they showed good work ethic and genuinely cared about kids.

I remember helping so many young ones around the Reality of the Situations they did not envision when first starting their careers. Some stuck it out and some just quit.

Before you start a career in Teaching or continue, this book is a good read that will help you realize you are not alone and prepare you for what you need to know and what you need to do.

I have written this in the familiar. I don't want it to look like, or sound like a text book. There is something here for everyone. You don't need to start at the beginning and drudge through it. Pick a chapter that catches your interest first.

I would hope that the Situations in this book jumpstart conversations among educators; some saying, " Yes, I know what she means here. I have had similar experiences and I have another helpful suggestion to share..." Well, DO just that! Share it with others! That is how we become good teachers. Make this book work for you so that one day you will look back and sing 'Thanks for the memories!"

TABLE OF CONTENTS

CHAPTER ONE

Situation: Teacher Training

So you can get a degree in poli-sci and then take a year's teacher training and become a teacher. That is how it seems. This may not seem a fair statement and I know that universities in our country really do try their best to prepare young people for this profession. Some universities are better than others. I am not going to get into an argument over this now but I will list some of the things needed to help teachers prepare for teaching in today's world. Are you prepared for the reality of this vocation? Hmmm, let's see…

I like the universities that put you into a practicum right away. It is shock reality. After a few weeks, for me it was 2 months, I knew this is what I wanted to do.

Practicums are the best reality check for this vocation and there should be lots of them. Make sure you get a good mentor teacher. Good ones are worth their weight in gold. Remember you owe it to yourself as you are paying for this training. Here is a reality, a situation….

For the most part I had great mentors…until my final practicum. I ended up in a Grade 4/5 class in a lovely suburb. It was a four month practicum from January to April. We didn't get March Break then. Great kids and a peppy mentor teacher. The reality was that after 2 months she became disgruntled with me and I could do nothing right. I was an emotional wreck. At one point she asked the Grade 6 teacher to come in and observe me. He was the PE jock in the school and came in casually in his sweats. He walked around for a bit and looked me over. Couldn't find anything wrong and said to my mentor, "Too perfect. She knew I was coming."

In the staffroom I was referred to as my mentors 'Problem.' Totally crushed, I almost gave it all up at that point. My wonderful boyfriend, now my husband, was a great support. The last week of class, the principal called me into the office and I was prepared to give up teaching if he told me to. However, he ended up thanking me for coming to the school and told me I had a bright future and a wonderful way with kids. I was stunned. What happened here?

Weepy, naive and confused I ended up talking to my university faculty associate. She was wonderful. She told me that I should have talked to her sooner. She said that the mentor teacher may have been envious of my youth, my spunk and my wealth of new ideas. This idea was the last thing I would have considered. Boy, did I ever live in a fairy tale world, eh?

There is an interesting ending to this story. Fifteen years later, I was an established teacher in an island school district. It was District Pro D Day and I was a presenter. I had gone to China with 80 educators and came back with a great talk and slide show. One of the Big Names that day was an expert on Discipline. I went to listen to him speak…OMG, he was the PE jock from that practicum! I introduced myself to him later in the day amid lots of congrats from colleagues on my efforts and the look on his face was worth it when I candidly said to him, "Be sure to tell my mentor that her 'Problem' made out all right!"

It takes 5 university years to become a teacher. Five work years lost and a lot of money in student loans. Even then, when you finish it will take you 10 years to reach maximum salary. That's the reality. Geez, why do this job then, when you can go to a lovely tech school, apprentice for a few years and reach a decent salary. Heck, I know a friend who became a Professional Cake Decorator and makes more money that I ever did!

It takes a Special Person to become a Teacher. You are considered a Professional. You need quite a Tool Box to be able to do this job! Education is not a factory job. It is not a business and should never be treated as such. It is basically an Institution of Relationships, Building Growth in People, one Child at a time.

Education is never constant. I loved it because it is always evolving and changing. Research is continually showing us how the brain works, how people learn, best practices for literacy and numeracy, a new breakthrough for teaching the autistic child or new ideas around Outdoor Education, new this or new that…. The learning is endless. As a professional, I always loved expanding my knowledge and Growing as a Person with my colleagues and my students. (True confession here: This is the One Thing I miss in retirement. Right now I am wondering, What is the new thinking? Are there new curriculum changes in the fall? Hmm? This, and not being around to watch the kids grow is often what I miss the most. Thank God, I have a lifetime of great memories.)

So more about Teacher Training. Methods courses will teach you the importance of time management, your voice, questioning techniques, how to give effective descriptive feedback, how to help kids reflect, assess their work using a myriad of developed criteria and rubrics. Good courses will show you the tricks to subject delivery so the material engages students and that is not as easy as it looks today. Kids who have grown up with TV's and DVD players in their rooms or with laptops, Ipads, Game Boys, DS's and other techy toys need new ways to become engaged. More on this later but learn as much as you can around best practices. Methods courses will teach you the importance of assessment both summative and formative. This is a biggy too! Methods will teach you about strategies around discipline and class control. This is another biggy for the toolbox.

Methods courses are important and valuable but really not the heart of your learning. You can read about reading strategies, class management and assessment, feel you are well organized and make lovely lesson plans that look good on paper but it isn't until you try it out, engage the kids with the subject, will you see how it all comes together. That said, your lovely lesson plan may work for one class quite well and then flop with another. I remember teaching a few high school Drama classes and I had spent a big chunk of time planning, what I thought were some very engaging lessons around Melodrama. The first class looked at me as if to say, "Duh? What? Are you kidding me?" So what did I do wrong? Not deliver it correctly? Next week I had a younger class who ate it up and couldn't get enough. They performed a cute melodrama and we all laughed like crazy until the end of term! Go figure!

I have come to learn in Education that teachers need to be trained for today's kids who live in a world very much different from 10 or 20 years ago. Times have changed since you were in school. Can you see the changes in your lifetime? Can you list them?

So here is the Philosophy according to Sharlene regarding Teacher Training today.

In the Ideal World I would like to see prospective teachers spend their five university years doing the following.

Number One - Taking a good first year of solid arts courses. Why?

The university life is often your first step away from home and self-discipline and self-regulation can be a hard lesson learned. Dealing with your personal values finding your way around parties, drinking, drugs, and sex and then there is the course work, which is why you are there. It can be hard, time consuming, lots of writing, and lots of research. Not all research can be found on line, Wikipedia or Google. Sometimes you just have to get out there and talk to people, and reflect. Now, isn't that a reality check for kids who have grown up in the instant information world and who communicate via text, online, Facebook etc.... lol!

You need to be able to actually converse with a myriad of professors, some of which will be interesting and engaging and some not. Some will not see you as the little bright kid who got straight A's in high school. They will see you as a number and a third year student will mark your work. You may be upset and wonder why? Go and find out! You paid for that course. Be diplomatic, not emotional. I did most of my post grad work as a young, working wife and mother sweating over a Correct-o Typewriter from 9 to 11 pm trying like hell to finish my essay via Distance Ed. I am not a super human but this taught me discipline and time management. It also taught me to communicate effectively. Here was my strategy. I would get my course work and feel Overwhelmed!

Distance Education courses put you through more requirements that regular university course work because they want to make sure you really GET the Learning Outcomes…that, or some Prof wants to impress you with what they know and you are expected to regurgitate their brilliance. (My sincere apologies to all the great thinkers and Profs out there. I do not mean you! Don't clog my inbox with hate mail.)

I made the effort to talk to the person who would be my mentor or tutor. That's right, T-A-L-K, not text. Today, I would Skype or Facetime. I took the time to ask questions about my assignments. I had a list of questions so I wasn't babbling. This first conversation usually gave me a clear idea what this marker was looking for. Some wanted the essay to look pretty. Some wanted lots of quotes. Some wanted length. Some wanted lots of research. But, the best prof/marker wanted you to THINK. They wanted you to interpret the material to fit you. This is the course you will learn from.

I remember my final Masters Course. It was to do with Educational Philosophy. The professor was a noted doctor in this subject. It was also June and school was winding down. Course work was due the end of July. This, along with classes. Pressure! I had to read 6 books, write an essay from each book and then combine them encompassing a final paper. I diligently read the books and took notes. I did the essays but had NO idea what to do for my final paper. I remember feeling tired, afraid of failure and absolutely clueless. I came close to the breaking point, when I finally had the chance to talk to my Prof (there is that work again…talk.) She asked me what books I liked best, and why, and what I wanted to explore more. She was asking me what I thought! She wanted me to think and reflect. Well, with her gentle guidance I did and I wrote a dynamite paper about kids and their emotions.

It is these wonderful teachers that make you think, and discover, that really make a difference. Those university years, when you are paying for your courses will show you good teachers. In turn, they will teach you what good teaching is.

That is the situation…

Number Two - Learn and practice Conflict Resolution. Why?

Simply put, because you will meet it and lots of it. Yes, we know you are brilliant and ready to change the world but there will be kids, parents, and colleagues who will not like you…for whatever the reason. It happens and I will talk about this in more detail in following chapters. In the meantime, it is your best interest to learn to meet conflict diplomatically and head on. Don't cringe or avoid it. It is a part of life. Live it, deal with it, learn from it and move on. Say it out loud. Like a mantra. Yes, the hurts are real and often relived at odd moments BUT turn it into a learning experience, write it down and tuck it into your Brag File.

Brag File?? That is where you collect all the meaningful things you get from kids, parents and colleagues. Just the most meaningful ones. It is nice to look through them from time to time. Not too many people will validate what a wonderful, caring educator you are SO establish that belief with the evidence you have.

If you screw up and make a mistake. Well, we all do. Just because you had a brain fart and told a child to Shut Up (oops) you are not a bad person. Don't bury it. Deal with it right away. Tell someone. Your Principal, fellow teacher, your spouse, a good friend. Apologize. Face it, deal with it, learn from it and move on. Is this strategy beginning to sound like a broken record? In dealing with it quickly, kids can be forgiving and understanding. It also shows that you are not absolute perfection either and that in facing it, you have modeled integrity.

People who are educational leaders; those who work in Human Resources everyday have something to teach you. These leaders and super teachers should talk to you about conflict.

Teachers need to learn to deal with conflict in a reasonable comfortable way. Is that an oxymoron? Well, it sure is the situation….

Number Three - Take effective Parenting Courses. Why?

Because there will be times where you may do more parenting that teaching. Sounds negative and I can hear my colleagues laughing I know, but it is a reality today with two parents working trying to make ends meet, often detached kids, split families, blended families, drugs, sexual knowledge way too young, undisciplined, no self-regulation ability, bullying, cyberbullying etc. You get the picture. It is nice to know

     -a little first aid. How to heal the hurt.

     -how to help a child through family dynamics; a split

      home or blended family

     -how to deal with death and the grieving process

-how to deal with anxiety and common fears

-how to deal with disclosures; everything from how to

be a friend to recognizing abuse

Working in the public sector you will be expected to be perfect, all knowing and wise. Don't laugh. People will look to you for the answers to the problems within their lives, especially kids. (i.e. Why does my mommy not come home at night? Why did daddy go away? Why did my dog die and where is he now? Why is my brother always sick in the hospital? etc....)

The people in Public Health, Family Resources and the Ministry of Children and Families are Earth Angels and should teach this part of your training. Who better than from those on the front line? Whether you are a parent or not - Put parenting skills into your tool box.

Number Four - Look after children outside of school time. Why?

Ok, I can hear some educators out there really laughing now at this but I think young people who may not have had children yet or perhaps were raised without siblings need to understand the entire process of child development. Yes, there are lots of good texts on this and videos I am sure, but I think it will help you understand child development better if you look after them beyond the hours of school.

I am **not** saying you need to have your own children to be a good teacher because I know some of the very best teachers I ever met didn't. I am saying that, IF you are serious about making a career working with children, then you need to understand and experience firsthand what goes into raising them. Teachers should understand a basic timeline of child development. For example, baby crying, diapers (input/output), common illnesses, vaccinations, teething, crawling, sitting, walking...and that is only the first year of life! The school day is one part of their growth, and granted, with some kids, you may spend more time with them than their parents. This part of the Ideal Teacher Training Program aligns itself with the previous one. Good parenting skills. In my time, I was given a great book called <u>The Mother's Almanac</u> (Marguerite Kelly & Ella Parsons, illustrated by Rebecca Hirsh, Broadway Books, NY, 1975, 1992). This book was written by 2 mothers who had eight children between them. They were not specialists but they gave me a picture of many stages of life. My daughter tells me that book is a bit outdated now so go get yourself the newest how-to, most-popular manual for raising kids. Tuck it into your Tool Box. You won't regret it.

Early Childhood Educators, Nurses, Family Resource personnel, Ministry of Children and Families agents, Teen Councilors and..oh!.. Mothers should deliver this training to you. But I also feel new teachers should be accountable for a specific number of hours of time (say 24?) looking and working with children beyond school time. This could be in the form of a preparing a Learning Log showing time spent, what you did and a good piece on reflection about what you have learned. Here are some ideas and I think university staff can help set these up easily. They can put together the contacts and do the legalities.

-volunteer at a Day Care

-visit and volunteer at a hospital for sick children

-live a short time with a family that fosters children

-become a Big Sister or Big Brother, take your little

    buddy to the park, dinner and a movie, hike and have

    a picnic, go swimming…

-volunteer and supervise youth at a Teen Center

-baby sit

You will see children at their best and at their worst. You will see them when they are happy, sad or sick. When you stay up all night with a kid with croup or even look after a kid with a cold, you will nag your class to put on their coats and mittens for the rest of your career!

If you already have children of your own, you can check off this box because you are nodding in agreement with me. You get it!

Does this make sense?? It's the reality of the situation….

Number Five - Learn about and work with Children with Special Needs. Why?

Sheesh…beyond kids whom I knew to be slow learners, I never thought in my 32 year career would I need to know how to deal with cerebral palsy with petit mal seizures, learn deaf sign, learn braille and be able to teach a visually impaired child soccer, or be prepared to deliver an epi-pen for a child with a severe life threatening peanut allergy, deal with epilepsy, help a child with Asperger's with socialization, or help a nonverbal student talk and sing using pic-symbols and a Big Mac Tape recorder or helping a child with Downs

Syndrome to read, or teaching a kid with Fetal Alcohol Syndrome or just trying to figure out the Autism Spectrum. How about Sanfilippo Syndrome Type A or Williams Syndrome or Hirschbrungs Disease or Gillian Barre Syndrome? Look these up on the internet. Three of them affected my own family and one affected the child of a very good friend.

Get the picture?

I remember taking one pretty dry, short and quick Learning Disabilities course. I definitely could have benefited with a better awareness of children with special needs.

You may never need to teach a child with a severe disability or have to learn any of the above BUT you need to be aware of the possibility. More importantly, you need to know where to go to help these children. The internet is a good source of information but also misinformation. TALK to an expert. Yes, talk. Try to be at least a little aware of the situation before that child enters your class. They deserve to learn and your dynamic job and that of your Special Education Team is to ensure and help that child perceive themselves as learners. It can be daunting but there is so much out there to help these kids. This is where technology such as laptops and Ipads are such helpful tools.

Often children with learning disabilities are the smartest ones. They already know they need to work harder than most. They may display behaviours and you can understand that because their world must seem like climbing mountain after mountain after mountain. These kids design their own coping strategies or they are taught them by professionals in the know. Every success, no matter how big or small is a celebration. I never worry about what will happen to them. In developing a hard work ethic, they take that attitude into the adult workplace. They survive. In contrast, think about the straight A student who is lucky enough to find learning easy all the way through school. How do you think this person copes when they come up against something they don't understand for the first time? I have seen that happen and it isn't pretty.

School counselors, Special Education teachers, Learning Assistance teachers, Learning Disability specialists and syndrome experts AND Parents of children with disabilities should teach this part of your preparedness for teaching. (I talk more about this later in the chapter on The Kids.) Working with these kids, young teens and adults too is a good way to help you visualize the scope of their lives.

Think about the disabilities you have had to overcome in your regularly somewhat normal life up to now. Mine was writing. Really! As you can see I don't follow all the correct grammar rules and I like to write in the familiar. Working with children with special needs will make you a better person. They will teach you; tolerance, patience, perseverance and an appreciation for life itself.

Number Six -Specialize - Find your niche   Why?

You should be allowed to take several elective courses to expand or upgrade your area of interest in education. Mine was music and drama. I also loved teaching Social Studies. If you have a specialty, you will most likely get hired. Districts are looking for teachers with expertise in music, computers, special education and work experience with kids with disabilities, counseling, physical education, outdoor education, and environmental education.

Music came easy to me. I learned to play three chords on the guitar (C, G and D7) and was able to play 100 songs easily. You can entertain primary children or bring out your electric guitar for the teenagers. E bay is a good way to buy a cheap guitar if you are going to take it to school and drag it along to campouts, field trips and school picnics.

Number Seven - Practicums and More Practicums.

I started this chapter talking about practicums and can't say enough about how important they are. A two week placement just doesn't seem long enough. A month at least. Experience all ages from primary to adults if you can.

Teachers are often so concerned with the methods they have learned and impressing their sponsor teachers. I remember so many young newbies coming to me with their impressive lesson plans. I looked them in the eye and flipped through them like a deck of cards and said, "Ok, in Lesson Plan 101 you have passed with flying colours. Beautiful work!" Now this was usually met with shock and some upset but really, am I going to mark the lesson plan that I know will either fly like magic or flop? Sheesh, I have prepared a lot of these. I gently explain that it is not how the lesson goes as much as it is something I call, Kid-Sense! That is what I will be watching...

Kid-Sense

This is the heart of teaching. It is how we work with, mingle, engage, treat, and come to love the children put in our care. There was a time where the belief was that I was responsible for the teaching and student the learning. The student need not like me because I was all knowing and their job was to learn. Wow…what a different world now. Thank goodness for this because, Gordon Neufeld & Gabor Mate state in their book, <u>Hold on to Your Kids: Why Parents Need to Matter More than their Peers, (Vintage Canada, Toronto,2004, 2013)</u>, that relationships matter more than ever! And they do.

A simple example of understanding Kid-Sense would be this: You are giving a great lesson and the kids are engaged. You have them sitting on the carpet for over a half an hour. Your lesson is good. Great visuals but they are getting squirmy and talking. Why? Well, you try sitting on that carpet for that length of time! Some kids can do it but most need to move. Get them up and moving, A-B partner talk, reflecting what they have learned… You get the picture?

Another example: Johnny is continually late for school and it may not be his fault. Do you need to show your frustration at the door when he arrives? No. Greet him with a smile and a kind word every time. If you did this for the 10 months you have him, he will never forget you. The late issue can be dealt with adult to adult, whether it is a phone call home or a talk with your principal and/or Home School Coordinator who can take it from there.

If you know now that you are not up to achieving a monster amount of Kid-Sense, then put this book down and pass it on to someone else. Really, I mean it! You need to bring out the inner-kid within yourself. To teach kids you have to become one and think at their level; try to perceive your lesson from their eyes. Come to know their likes, their dislikes, their music, what's cool and what's not, their fears, their emotions, play their games, learn silly jokes and sillier songs, do string tricks, yo-yo, play skipping games or talk like Donald Duck.

This ability is needed if you are teaching Kindergarten or teenagers.

Let me clarify that having Kid-Sense is not being their buddy. You are still the adult and the appropriate boundaries of trust and authority apply. This may be an old fashion idea but I still think it is important to have children call you by your formal name, that is, you being a Mr., Mrs., Miss or Ms....I think this because it not only defines that boundary between you and your students, it is a sign of Respect and in this world I found that Respect is something hard to earn and quick to lose.

Kid-Sense is again, perceiving the world through the eyes of the child.   Kids need to make attachments and you will be a significant one in their lifetime. You have your students for ten months. Show your Kid-sense on a daily basis. Make the most of it and don't waste a day. Those kids will not forget you.

Final Thought - Take advantage of anything that looks like Professional Development.

Especially if it is free. If it is not what you need you can politely bow out but you want your tool box stacked with as much as you can before walking into your first job. If you think of yourself as a life learner then you had better walk the walk. Professional Development is just that. It develops you as a professional.

I organized Professional Development days for both my school and the whole district. It is hard to please everyone, especially high school teachers. I found Pro D to be defined in two ways. Bear with me here.

- Personal-Professional Development. This is simply expanding You as a person. Stepping outside your comfort zone. Taking a workshop on Aboriginal Learning or Birdwatching in your area. How about something scary techy like using Ipads effectively, or making films with kids? Visit somewhere locally you haven't been like an historical site or a park. High school teachers often don't see this as Pro D. (Sorry, guys but it is true. I heard many of them say "This is not for me. I am not going to learn about Aboriginal Basket Weaving. I have better ways to use my time.)

But I feel, that expanding your experiences as a person, can help you find a lesson in it for kids. Ok, so here's an example. You go to Mexico on vacation, visit the sites and come back with some great pictures. Doesn't that inspire you to take a small teachable moment in time to show your students a few of those pictures on PowerPoint. Yes, the pretty sunsets are great and we can leave out the one of you at Jimmy Buffet's MargueritaVille Bar... but how about the people, the children, their school, the marketplace, the Aztec history. Pictures can engage kids into thinking and asking so many questions, especially kids who may not get a chance to have a vacation like that. Think of all the curriculum subjects that can be covered with your picture presentation.

During one of my final years in education, as principal of a small rural school, I left for 3 weeks in September to go to England. Our daughter was to have our first grandchild. The kids at school were bewildered as to why I left at the beginning of their year and where was England? As far as they were concerned it could have been Mars! When I returned I put together a short PowerPoint presentation in library time showing where England was, a little about the country where our Queen lives and they were thrilled!

There is something to be said about Personal Professional Development so suck it up, kiddo!

- <u>Professional-Professional Development</u>. This is simply an educational workshop that interests you or fits your class. In continuing to pick on high school teachers, this is what they usually look for on Pro D days. Something that fits their subject area. The best ones are those that give you something you can take and use in your class right away. Even if it is just one good new idea. And often you may be able to add to the workshop with an idea you have.

The boring workshops are those that give you mounds of philosophy and/ or background but never tell you how to apply the concept. You come away with more questions than answers and some confusion.

The Great Workshops may include things like

-Expanding New Ideas for your Art Class

-A New Math Strategy that Works

-Making Social Studies Come Alive

-Teaching Multi-Grade Levels

-Science Outside

-Teaching French through Drama

See what I mean? My advice is to suck up as many workshops as you can. Boring or not!

At the end of the Professional Development Day there is usually a suggestion box. Now it would be a Monkey Survey on line today. The one comment that kept coming up time after time throughout my career was, "Wish I had more time to share with other teachers." So Right! I remember being a Grade 4/5 teacher within our district and it was nice to get together with other intermediate teachers and find out how they were doing or how they were teaching this or that. Poof! Then the day was over and I was back to my family and my job.

In short, Teachers Need to SHARE! That is how we become great teachers. Often parents and sometimes our colleagues will look at our amazing classes and think we are all independently brilliant at teaching every single subject. Not so. It goes back to that Tool Box. We become great teachers with brilliant ideas by learning from others and copying their ideas. Elementary teachers are always doing this, sharing ideas or files in staffroom conversations. High school teachers talk within their Subject Team Meetings.

I took a notebook into every workshop or school or class I went into. I wrote down great ideas I saw on the walls and/or I talked to teachers. I had boxes upon boxes of files on every subject I taught. My poor husband can testify to this when he built me floor to ceiling shelves in one room of our house. Nowadays, a phone camera or tablet device can handily take pictures anytime, anywhere. It can record good lectures and you can film good lessons. You can store assignments, worksheets…anything on an external drive to your computer (like I am doing for this book). I know one new teacher who has a set of Flash Drives colour coded for each subject she teaches. And you can find a wealth of teaching best practices on the internet. Sure cuts down on the paper files, the posters and the visual aids you will collect. Most of you may already know this. The techy world still amazes me and I try to keep up to what is new, even if only to impress my own kids. Ha!

Share. Learn. Copy it. Record it. Film it. Save it. Use it. Share it! See how that came full circle? Sharing is the Talking Part with other teachers. Take the time to talk face to face. Ok, today if it is not in the staffroom, I would Skype or Facetime with fellow teachers.

Easy Peasy and that's the situation that makes you a better than Great Teacher…

CHAPTER TWO

Situation: You're a Teacher at Last!

You are a Professional Teacher and the world is waiting for you. Teachers are needed in all corners of the world. Five university years of hard work have come and gone and you feel ready. But are you?

<u>Situation: What is your Vision?</u>

Some may call this your Belief Statement but I like the word Vision. What are your expectations of yourself as a teacher in today's world? Given your experience at this point in time or whether you have been teaching for several years, I think you need to formulate a vision of why you are doing what you are doing. It is like a mantra; a guide you live by, something you can say to yourself when you need to during the ups and downs.

I kept mine simple:

"I care deeply about the individuality of each child.

I never want to act or make a decision without first asking the question, "Is this what's best for kids?"

This guided me through my career.

I never lost sight of the first part. Each child was different and should be respected as such. You may think you know it all about kids but one will come along who will challenge you to the core and teach you a lot about yourself. This I found true right up to my final year.

The latter part of my vision was a constant guide in helping me plan for my year. It also helped with discipline issues and other school dynamics. It forced me do some real soul searching during times like Teacher Strike. Was I doing what was best for kids? Or when working in a small school, having to make difficult decisions around staffing formulas as per government regulations, may not have been the best class composition for kids, but it was the best I could do. If I could say that I was honestly doing my best and putting kids first, I felt I was living up to my Vision.

So…. before you begin, formulate your vision and put it where you can see it. It might be on your desk pad or on your fridge or in permanent felt marker on your bathroom mirror.

Skim over the titles in the rest of this chapter to see what applies or appeals to you. Here I will divulge some inside secrets or as my friends would say, the Philosophy according to Sharlene.   Shshsh…

Situation: Getting a Teaching Job 101

Depending where you live or where you want to work, depending on your family dynamics, and/or depending on your financial situation, it can often be a challenge landing the job you want. Hopefully your training or experience adequately prepared you for the search.

- Teacher On Call or TOC-ing Now the internet can carry your profile and resume anywhere you want it to go. That is a great way to reach a lot of places. If you are willing to go to remote areas you will most likely get a job easier than you will in the larger towns and cities. Most teachers like to work in popular urban areas. If this is you, be prepared to dig in and wait. There may be a surplus of teachers and even then you will most likely need to jump hoops to get on the substitute list, known in my area as the Teacher On Call List.

TOC-ing is a good way to start if your situation enables you to do this. If you are new to the profession it will give you experience across many grade levels that you may not have had in your practicums. It can also help you find the grades or subjects you would like to spend your career. I started out as a primary teacher but fell in love with Grades 4 to 7. Later I taught some junior high Science, Social Studies and Fine Arts and that was fun too.

I am sure you know the rudiments of introducing yourself to the class and establishing mutual respect, the Class Goal of the Day…blah blah blah… But here are some secrets that helped me recognize TOC's from the teacher and the principal's perspective….

Secrets:

-Come and visit and show your face. It is good to call the secretary first to let the school know you would like to come for a short visit. Also nice for you to know that the school is not out on a field trip or the principal away. The end of the day is best. As a principal, I really appreciated it when I knew you were coming. Make it short and sweet. "Hi, My name is _____. I am new to the area. I would like the opportunity to teach in your school. Here is my card. Thanks. May I have a quick look around?" You will most likely get a "Yes" here if we knew you were coming. This will give you a chance to poke your head into a few classes and talk to some teachers.

As principal, I always took the time to meet new people and I pinned up the card on my board. If I knew you were coming I would put that information up on the morning information board. Putting a face to your name is a good idea.

-Did you get the part about leaving a card? You may already know this but it is good to have your picture on it. Again, if I am meeting several new TOC's, I want to be able to put the face to the name and remember the communication we had. Also make sure your contact info is up to date. So many times I called you and the number was wrong or out of service….

-If you are on the TOC list and able to get to the school early enough ASK someone about the class, especially if there is something specific about a student. If the principal and other teachers are getting busy for the day, ask the secretary. She knows everything. It is worth it to know that you are going into a class with a difficult student, a bullying problem, a recent death….This way you will know how best to use the next secret.

-Have a Tool Box of Tricks. You may need to run at a moment's notice and you need to be prepared for anything. Anything, means anything from 'The teacher will be away for one day. Her plan is on her desk.' to ' The teacher has had to face a personal traumatic situation and we may need you for a week or longer. There is no plan at this time.' For a short term you may need to be Super Teacher, a subhuman creature! Hahaha!

I always looked over the plan and spent the first 15 minutes if I could by playing introductory games like Group Juggle, Whole Class Skipping (I bought a long piece of good boat rope for this) or just Hot Potato with a Ball that lights up. (You can find these at a Dollar Store.) I would take them outside if I could, or to the gym or I would clear the desks back for a bit. Why do this? Well, when kids enter class each day, they come as a mixture of emotional levels. Some you see clearly, most you don't. If you take the time to introduce yourself, set the Class Goal of the Day and then go somewhere for physical play, it is amazing how they all come back to class ready to go…

I always took my guitar too. Kids of all ages are fascinated by them and like to watch you play. It is good to transition between subjects or take 10 minutes to sing' Purple People Eater', and the like, right after lunch before the rest of the day. Like I said earlier, if you learn 3 chords you can play 100 silly songs and I collected some good ones even teenager's love. Email me and I will pass them along to you.

A bag of silly joke books is good to collect too. I found a lot of mine at Thrift Stores or school book order forms. I never made a big deal about them but would casually say something like," When you are finished you assignment, I have some joke books at the back table you might like to look at." Not making a big deal about it was a cool invite and sooner or later giggles would ensue. Even poor readers are willing to try a joke or two.

If you have a good trick, be sure to share it with your colleagues! These are just a few of my favourite tricks I used successfully.

-I always had a small bag of simple toys like tops, yoyos, skipping ropes, cars for the sandbox, juggling balls, etc. I picked them up at Dollar Stores and replaced them as they broke. When I went to Mexico one year, I brought back a lot of wooden tops and ball-in-a-cup toys and spinning spool on string. I would take these out with me on recess or lunch duty and kids of all ages came running. My rule was to just let me know if one broke (cheap so no big deal) and please return them at bell time. If you are TOCing, kids will remember you!

-Always leave the class in good order. I know you most likely were told this BUT it is amazing how many TOC's leave quickly and the class messy, the marking not done, no notes for the teacher and not a plan for the next day. As a principal, I would hear about these complaints from my teachers. On the other hand, if you went out of your way to do the above, plus asked if there was anything else you could do, like help with an extra-curricular sport activity at lunch or after school… WE will remember YOU and don't forget to leave your card!

-School districts have a habit of hiring their TOC's. Why? Simply because we know you and if you are that Really Diligent One with the Bag of Tricks, you can often ask the teachers or the principals you worked for to be a reference for you.

A final word about TOC-ing. I have said you need to be Super Teacher but in reality the situation you find yourself in may be a difficult one and all your tricks and strategies may not work. If you are doing your best, then that is all you can do. As principal, I always told my TOC's to come to me if they need to. Do not leave the class; just ask a reliable student to come and get me. It is good to nip something in the bud before it gets out of hand. I know you want to impress and do your best but asking for help is not a reflection of your teaching ability. It is a reflection of your seriousness about the job you are doing. Enough said.

Your Resume

Now I am sure the university prepared you for this. You have your cover letter, your education, your experience, your references, your hobbies. You put it up on an internet website that school districts go to. You make nice paper copies to mail to districts. Blah blah blah..

You put a lot of work into it because your job potential depends on it. Right?

As a principal who sat on a few hiring committees and personally hired teachers for the school, let me share some secrets. These are personal secrets from me to you. Some of my colleagues in education may not agree with some of this, so take what you think will work for you.

Secrets:

-Don't spend a lot of time on your cover letter. A teacher I recently talked to told me that the cover letter was really stressed at her university. Ok, but.... When you are looking through a lot of resumes, cover letters all sound the same. " I like kids....I am a team player...I am enthusiastic...I am a lifelong learner....I work hard....I take being a teacher seriously..." So, make it as novel as you can and keep it short and sweet.

-Make sure your contact information is correct and I can get a hold of you quickly. This includes your address, your phone numbers - cell and land line, work number, email address, blog site if you have one. I had one teacher who put her mother's cell number and that is how I got a hold of her. Mothers have a way of moving mountains to let you know someone is interested in you.

-The same goes for your references. If I am interested in you, I want to talk to them as soon as I can. I usually like to call two and sometimes three references. Give me at least 2 numbers and an email address for each.

Again, like a broken record, make sure the information is correct! Make sure your references know they might be called. I am sure you were told to do that but many don't and the reference is often shocked at my call, feeling awkward. I have lost interest about then...

Make sure your references names and titles are correct.

>-Mrs. Jones, Primary Teacher, Somewhere School, School District ..

>-Mr. Smith, Principal, 2000-2012 Somewhere School, School Dist...., Presently Retired

-Big Secret here>>After your name and contact information, tell me everything you can do that can be used in your class room!!! I will check your experience next and after that your education but if I am looking for a primary teacher, I am going to look for that right away.

Use list form, something like this

> -I can teach all elementary grades. Most experience at the Primary levels.
>
> -I know BIG SMART Reading Strategies
>
> -I am trained in Fancy Math concepts
>
> -I am proficient with computers (MS Office, Word, Excel, Publisher, PowerPoint, Windows Movie Maker)
>
> -I can use a Smart Board, Ipads and a document camera for instruction.
>
> -I took two Special Education courses in university dealing with student learning disabilities.
>
> -I play the guitar and can lead singing with students.
>
> -I speak French.
>
> -I have a PE background, specifically gymnastics and swimming instruction
>
> -I have Level One First Aid certification, Food Safe Certification
>
> -Taught the Rock Solid, anti-bullying WITS program
>
> -Science Wild Certification - teaching outdoor education.
>
> -I worked with a team of teachers on a staff development inquiry project entitled, 'Does helping

primary students create images improve their writing ability?"

Listing your credits is a credit to you! This is no time to be modest. Make sure you mention every significant workshop you take. It can be impressive. It will get the attention of your employer right away and if I want clarification about something, I know how to get a hold of you right away…right?

-Last secret is a controversial one but I will tell you anyway. Include a picture if you can. Not like your passport photo but I always included a one good picture of me; usually the one that is annually taken at school, and I included a page collage of me working with kids. If you are a principal looking through a lot of resumes this helps. I spent one summer trying to hire a French, Social Studies teacher for a junior high school. I looked at soooooo many resumes but came back to the ones I could read clearly and quickly. A picture gave me a reference point. And if I am talking to you, as I was that summer to a young teacher across the country willing to come to our little town, it was nice to put a face to the name. I hired her and she was great!

- • The Interview

Yeah! You got short listed. If you used the tricks I mentioned above you will have a good chance of getting an interview. Interviews come in several forms. Might be simply the principal in their office at the school or you could face a panel of administrators hiring for the next school year. Hopefully someone has helped you with the interview process. You don't need to be a new teacher to know this. Some of this may seem common sense but when you are doing a lot of interviews in one day, these are the things that I noticed…Here are some more Secrets…

-Look Smart! I mean, look the way you would if you were to join my staff. Sit straight, introduce yourself and shake all hands firmly. Make eye contact. Talk clearly. I know this sounds like "yah..yah…yah" but it's amazing the people who I have had to ask to speak up, who peer over their glasses, who slouch, and who do NOT look confident.

-This is No Time to Be Modest!! This interview is all about YOU and how wonderful you are so convince me you are the person I need. I noticed that women are a lot more modest at interviews than men. Men can usually talk easily about themselves. So Don't Be Modest, ladies!   Again, have that 'What I Can Do List' memorized that is a part of your resume. I want to hear that. A lot of teachers bring copies of their work with kids and achievements. Do this and leave a copy if you can. We most likely will have a chance to look through it later.

-Almost all interviews will want to know your knowledge around assessment (formative and summative) as well as discipline practices and curriculum.

-Usually at the end of the interview you will have a chance to add something. If you haven't already, this would be a good time to speak about your Vision of Teaching. This is something that drives you; it is the core of why you want to teach.

-Also, talk at some point, briefly about your future as a teacher. Something like

-After several years' experience with primary grades, I would like to be involved in a literacy best practices group.

-I would like to make an effort to get together with other Science Teachers within your district to share ideas.

-I would like to be a teacher leader in Special Education one day here.

These are good because the employer sees that not only do you have a Vision for Teaching but you have just described yourself as a lifelong learner without saying it. Employers like to see a positive leader. That's a real big secret!

One final word about the Interview: You may be brilliant but you didn't get the job. This can be discouraging. I know this well from both sides of the desk. Here are two things to understand.

#1. You never get to see what the other candidates bring to the interview. Time and time again, I told discouraged teachers this and I am unable to disclose information about the other interviews I did. I know you are sad but don't give up! Don't assume you interviewed poorly, or that you are not good enough. And be careful you don't vocalize your disappointment in negative terms like, "The district doesn't like me." This is just emotion speaking. Not a teacher I would want if I heard it.

#2. What can you do??? Go back to the source! See if you can talk to the administrator or someone on the panel about your interview. How can I improve? What advice can you give me to interview better or is there an area of my teaching experience I need to upgrade? I have done this myself, even over the phone, and it paid off! Again, like at your interview, you are projecting a positive, polite image of yourself. I always ended this conversation with a Thank You for the opportunity to talk. Simple manners go a long way.

Best of luck!

CHAPTER THREE

Situation: I Got A Job!

Wisest words I ever heard were "You never get a second chance to make a first impression." I sure remembered that going into every job I had.

Public Perception

I never told people I was a teacher unless they asked specifically. Why? ...here's the situation. I am proud to be an educator but the general public is often intimidated by the fact that you have a lot of education and people come with varying perceptions of school from their own positive and often negative experiences. So many times when I told people I was a teacher they would take up a lot of time talking about

> "Isn't it horrible about what is happening in our schools today....." or

> "Let me tell you about when I went to school..." or

> "My kid's problems at school are..."

People remember the negative experiences mostly. I do. I remember well the bullies who called me names, the teacher who hurt my feelings in PE. These stay with you. It is a good thing though that the positive experiences far outweigh the negative for me. The point here is, that the public are often intimidated by you because you are an educator and a professional. It is that simple.

Therefore, be as down to earth as you can with your parents. Read that line again because it is a real key to successfully making that first impression. Here are some tricks you may or may not know....

-Have parents call you by your first name. "Hi, Mrs. Johnson. I am happy to be Mary's teacher this year. Please call me Sharlene. The kids call me Mrs. Scofield."

-Meet and greet whenever you can, that is, in the parking lot, at bus time, in the hall at the beginning of the day when you are greeting the students at the door and also again at the end of the day. Take time to be visible within the community, stop and talk casually with parents you see.

-If you are new to the school and community. Take the time to step back and be visible and listen. What is important in the community? What are the traditions? Use this information in your class room wisely.

-The first week of school, before your September class meeting or open house, CALL EACH PARENT. Start off something like this..

"Hi, Mrs. Johnson, this is Sharlene Scofield calling, Mary's teacher? I am calling because I like to touch base with the moms because I know you are the best expert about Mary and I was wondering if there is anything you think I need to know. "

You have no idea how this will jumpstart a conversation that will give you a lot of information about children, some of which may be quite personal.

-"I don't live with Mary's father."

-"My child still wets the bed each day."

-"My son was abused at an earlier age."

-My son loves science and learning about dinosaurs."

-If you can make a connection to sports, my daughter will learn."

You will learn things about families and homes that may shock you or make you smile. Either way, you will have some inside information about the home that will help you understand each child. File the info away carefully and confidentially.

End the conversation, no matter how long or short it is, by giving the parent your home phone number. Some of you may or may not agree but I think that if one of my students goes home and has a meltdown about something that happened, I would like my parents to be comfortable enough to call me and discuss it. Parents with concerns are parents that care. I would much rather have parents talk to me directly than behind my back.

September Talk.. First meeting with your parents.

This poem is timeless but says it all. Recite it to your parents…Send it in a class newsletter or your class handbook…Share it with others…

UNITY

I dreamed I stood
in a studio
And watched two
sculptors there.
The clay they used
was a young child's mind
And they fashioned it with care.

One was a Teacher
the tools she used
were books and
music and art;
One was a Parent
with a guiding hand
and a gentle loving heart.
And when at last
their work was done
They were proud of
what they had wrought,
For the things they
had worked into the child
could never be
sold or bought.
And each agreed she
would have failed
if she had worked alone,
For behind the parent
stood the school,
and behind the teacher
stood the home.

~Unknown Author

I always liked to take the time to talk with my parents in September whether your new school has scheduled class meetings, an Open House or not. This is a good idea. Some parents may not come but those that do, will be glad they did.

I put together a hand out for them and sent it home to those families that didn't come.

I talk and dress casually. I started my chat saying we are the Home and School Team. We need to work together to help your child have a successful year. Again, I tell them that I understand that they are the best experts regarding their child. Teach me what I need to know.

With parents I review......

-the daily routine

-behaviour contract (made with and by the students). I had it visible on the wall.

-curriculum issues. "This is how I teach math.".."The reading strategy I like best is.."

In my Handout, I would give my parents a short version of my yearly overviews in all subjects. Why? Well, if you need to do this for your principal, why not the taxpayer? This idea really helped me working in a small transient town. We always had new families putting their time in isolation for one or two years. Several parents thought that their kids were not getting a first class education because they were far away from the city. My overviews let them know that I am following the prescribed guidelines and when, during the year, I chose to teach them. This helped dispel the comment that "My child is behind in math because she lived up north..." No,...the overview I gave the parent noted that I chose to teach fractions and decimals in February, whereas the new school Mary went to in March had already taught this concept in November." Yes, Mary is behind but it is a matter of when the two teachers decide to cover this concept. This also applies to novel studies, Social Studies or Science units. In today's curriculum, teachers have many choices within a grade. You are a super hero if you cover them all. I found that my students from the northern community I worked in were often farther ahead because we had multi-grade splits and the kids learned from the grade ahead of them. Skills were reinforced when they taught the younger ones. Explain this to your parents.

Also, in my class handout, I included pictures of myself and kids from the previous year. Visuals can often say more than words, I think.

Also, I included some student evaluation of ME. Yes, ME! At the end of each year, usually the last day, I had students candidly write a report card about their year. They could be honest and anonymous. I put these evaluations in a sealed envelope to review in the summer. I asked them to tell me what I needed to tell next year's students. What did you like? What needs improving? Think about this. If WE are made to evaluate students, then aren't they the best judge of how we are doing? So, I added a few lines of student evaluation of Me in my Class Handbook. I kept it light and humorous. "She tells good jokes!" or "She's good with a yoyo."

An Aside here…I remember another comment that became my favourite. "When she gets mad..she's not really mad." I would be firm then lighten up quick when I felt angry. I also got very quiet and resorted to deaf sign. They would listen then. Learn to say with your hands, "Please sit down and be quiet. Now, right now. Thank you and listen. Thank you."

And further around this comment…I tried to debug the perception of YELLING in my classroom and that is a word that is misused among kids and parents. Because the perception between the two is as wide as an ocean! If a student says his teacher Yelled at him, it most likely is because he was asked several times to do something and didn't like it. Here, yelling = nagging to finish his work. But the parent hears this and the perception is that the teacher raised her voice and scared their child. Hmmmmm I simply told my students AND my parents that I don't yell, and if I do, then they could yell back! This always got a positive reaction from both especially if they knew this upfront from day one.

Some other comments I remember (and took note of) were

"She needs to write neater on the board and slow down." (The kid was right! I often write fast and messy when I'm trying to get a point across while talking too fast…..)

"Her voice gets louder when she is excited about something. Lower it." (Very good for me to know! I introduced The Wave after this comment. Quietly waving at me from your desk will tell me I'm a bit too loud. I practiced this with kids and made sure they knew it was ok to tell me this.)

-Homework expectations. Here I told my parents that I do not give homework for the sake of homework. It is a way to reinforce concepts missed or needing extra practice, or work needing to be finished. I always told parents to call me if there was a meltdown at home in the evening around homework or I asked them to simply put their initials at the top of the page and have the child show me the next day. This child I would make the effort to get to as soon as possible, even if it is over recess or lunch.

I liked working in schools where the students purchased school agendas. A note went home every day from the students saying what they had learned or homework to be done and was signed by the parents. If your school does not have these, you can use primary half books or a scribbler. When talking about this to parents, I asked them to take the time to write positive comments to their children about work done!

Also, I asked parents to let me know if the child will be away for long periods of time. Not all homework is written. A lot of class learning is through discussion and discovery but if the child is going on a family holiday, work can be put together so concepts are not missed. Simple things like extra reading or math work, or writing a travel journal. Explain that if you do that, you expect the work to be done too. Again, saying that we are partners right?

-the Visible Things. These are the field trips and/or extra-curricular activities you have planned. I would talk about this after the curriculum discussion. The extras are what parents like to see, really appreciate and understand. Show them your strengths whether it be musical, PE or outdoor education.

-I always reinforced the Teacher-Parent Team idea over and over... I ended the meeting with the importance of Good Communication being essential between home and school. Don't assume anything about me and I won't about you. I actually made a point of saying, "Don't believe everything you'll hear that happens at school and I won't believe everything I hear that happens at home." This always gets a wide eyed look from parents. I tell them that I will know a lot about your home this year, like when you party, when you fight, even though you tell them not to say anything. They do.

Also, "You can tell what kind of a day at school your child had by the way they come home...well, I meet and greet the children every morning and I can tell how you sent them." If I have a concern, I will call you and ask that you do the same. (This is why I do not mind handing parents my phone number. As a teacher, if you can reduce any school related stress at home, it sure cuts down small assumptions growing into mountains and hurt feelings.) I tell parents that if I am out to leave a message. I will call as soon as I can. I am serious about this and tell them that I do not use my answering machine to screen calls. Make sure your phone number is on the handout. I also gave it to my students and let them know they could call before 9 pm if they needed help. This was my situation and it worked!

I explain to parents that I will almost always stick up for them (barring abuse or any legality issues). Kids may often play home against school, much like they play parent against parent at times. I will not listen to any rude disrespect about parents...like "My mum is so dumb, she won't let me go on that sleep over.." or "My dad sucks because he won't buy a new car...." When I hear comments within the school like this, I pull the child aside and explain that this is rude and I don't want to hear it. I simply tell the child that I may not know your parents very well but I do know two things for sure. #1 - They love you a lot. #2 - They gave you life, and for that reason you owe them love and respect. Instead of being rude, talk to them diplomatically......Giving this example to parents, I tell them that I would appreciate the same respect. Again, call me ANYTIME if you have a concern, is the message to parents here. Remember, parents that call are parents that care.

<<<<RE: Social media and parents.. Be careful as to how you talk about school. >>> During the last 10 years of my

career, social media had become a way of life for us all. We enjoy communicating with family and friends, near and far. The public will talk about the school and always has …at the bus stop, over coffee, in the parking lot… BUT putting it up on social media is dangerous. Not only has it the potential to be hurtful but it can come with legal problems if names are mentioned. I also taught computer safety to students and I told them to remember 2 things. #1 When you are online, you are open to the world! And #2 There is NO such thing as Delete forever. It's nice to tell parents this too. Parents were aware of my school email address and I didn't mind them using it.

BUT…saying that, if there is a concern, a phone call is good to get and a face to face conversation is best!

-Invite parents into your class. In some areas this may conflict with union issues BUT parents have a right to be in the classroom. I would tell them when the best times were to help with art or center time…. whatever.

 Parents welcomed into your class are good insurance for you! Here is the Situation……When I first moved to a small isolated community, the common talk in the town was around a young teacher who was "No good"; "She liked the good kids and didn't help the weaker ones." I was shocked at this maliciousness and that teacher was gone by Easter time. I never told but a few what I did for a living for seven years. I had two children and that kept me quite busy. At the end of those years I was ready to return to the classroom and did some hard thinking as to how I could prevent malicious town talk about me. I did three things that worked

> #1 - The September Talk mentioned above, with the overviews and phone number

#2 - I wanted a volunteer parent in my class every day, even for one hour if possible. These parents could tell others, if needed, about 'how you were with the kids in the classroom.'

#3 – I sent a weekly newsletter home on Friday either written by me or the kids. We called it, The Pencil Gazette. It was short and sweet. I divided it into 3 sections. Class News like, "We started long division this week", then Kid News like, " John shot his first deer this week with his dad", then something funny like a cute joke (and I had a reading corner full of silly joke books.)

I also made sure the principal got a copy of each week's newsletter. I kept a copy of them on a pegboard. Now sometimes a student would tell me that their parents never read it and one told me that her mom used it to start the wood fire...hmmmm. Well, these parents can NEVER say they do not know what is going on in your classroom, right??

Today, there are more modern ways to connect with parents. Our grandson lives in New Zealand and his teachers use a really cool app that allows his parents and us to visually see (and comment) about what he is learning. It truly amazes me as we get to look inside his classroom half way around the world!

CHAPTER FOUR:

Situation: Priorities

The responsibility of being a teacher can be overwhelming! Soooo much responsibility lies with the decisions you make each day around the curriculum, field trips, students and discipline, staff/union issues, politics, parents.....

First Priority

The first priority is YOU! Yes, you!

You must be on top of your game every day at school. Sounds impossible, right? And, yes, it is impossible! There is no way you are able to be a Super Human but the public might think so. Remember that Education is not a business; it is an Institution of Relationships and good relationships really matter!

As I said, your first priority is YOU and that means your physical and mental health. No matter how many years you are teaching this will always be your first priority. Why? Simply because, if you are not reasonably happy and healthy, you cannot teach.

If you are sick, stay home! I always encouraged my teachers to have an emergency envelop with basic reading and math concept review that could be utilized when illness strikes. Include a copy of your overviews too in case you are away for the long term. The public will not thank you for coming to school sick. Your students will though.

Mental illness is real....but often misunderstood because it is not as visible as something like cancer. Depression or anxiety may (or may not) occur at any time within your career. We may not always see the change in ourselves but our family and colleagues will and so it follows your students will too. Go to the doctor. Deal with it. Sometimes it takes a few different 'happy pills' to figure out what works best for you. Also, your district will usually offer a confidential counseling service. Use it if you need to. Sometimes talking to a third party is helpful and sure saves you bending the ears of your spouse. I have been here and come out on top of my game.

Second and Third Priority

The second priority is your family. If they need you, be there. I cannot work knowing my own kids are sick at home or with a sitter, or your husband needs you or that your mother is seriously ill. Easier said than done, however and not always a reality. I have known some real amazing Super Heroes in teaching who have worked at school all day and then gone home to an ailing husband or terminally ill child. One told me it was the children at school who made her day and brought cheer to her life. These people live on hope and become stronger and more empathetic to families and the needs of others.

The third priority is your job if you are able to fulfill the first two priorities mentioned above. The public is paying you a good wage to do the very best with their children. They do not want to hear you complain or say that you've had a Bad Day. I found that parents would ask me this though. My answer was always A-B-C…that is, my day is Always Busy and Challenging. Say this with a smile!

Situation: What about those days when it is less than perfect! You screwed up! You raised your voice a bit too loud. You didn't have a good day. This is a reality and happens to us all. TALK to someone before you leave the school if you can, hopefully with an understanding principal. I always told my teachers they could vent with me and say anything they needed to behind the office door. I was there to help and support them. Venting is good therapy. It is helpful to talk with a teacher mentor too. They understand. Again.... TALK about what is bothering you with someone you trust. - DON'T hold it in. BE CAREFUL of public perception.

A quick word about Work Ethic

This is the situation. As I grew older I noticed that some teachers worked less beyond the class, especially those new to the profession. I remember one teacher saying to me," I can't do this marking because it is the weekend." And this was a district assessment expected to be done by a certain time. Sheeeesh... I was shocked! What happened here?

I remember spending hours after school and often weekends and evenings preparing for the day, week or month ahead organizing units and resources. Especially during the first few years of my career. Maybe it is simply easier to Google what you need now and find what you need on the internet. That sure would have saved time for me years ago.

And as I said, earlier, it is important to put you and family first...but

That said, for Priority #3, you will still need to put in some extra time planning or displaying work. I think it is important to engage kids as soon as they enter your room. Good displays, up to date marking, visible student work does this and I believe this to be true whether you teach Kindergarten or high school physics.

You are being paid a monthly salary, not an hourly one. Take the time to make sure you are well prepared for the job. I often did this in the summer time. I planned my Science and Social Studies units when I had lots of time to gather, look at or talk about new ideas.

Extra-Curricular Activities....Do you have to do this? The simple answer is YES, but you don't have to do everything!! Ensuring that Priorities One and Two are met, dive in and get going. Take on something that you are good at whether it be a school club, something musical or sports. It could happen before school, during recess or lunch or after school...whatever fits You, the kids and your school.

WHY do you have to do something extra-curricular? Simply put; you are not paid hourly and if you have a good helping of Kid Sense you will already know that you are a teacher that sees the child as a whole and that includes being involved with them outside of the classroom. (They get to see another side of you too, usually the FUN side.) In summary here, be mindful of your commitment to students, You being part of a school community and Your teacher group or union expectations.

A good work ethic, the extra effort you put into organizing your class, and doing something extra-curricular will be appreciated and noted.

CHAPTER Five:

Situation: Your Teaching World One Bite At a Time!

The Community

Where ever you live and teach… GET TO KNOW that community, especially if you are new to it! Do not rush in as the newbie in town and the Big Educator Expert. Be humble and gracious. Listen and observe. Be visible at community functions whether it is a simple potluck or important town meeting. Does your community value education? This seems negative but I have worked with in some areas where I felt I was a nuisance. What motivates people here? What do they value?

Here's the difference. In one small community I worked in, if you were a new face in town, everyone liked you and wanted to get to know you…then later if you turned out to be opinionated, negative or critical, people would drift away and leave you alone. In another community I worked in, the opposite was true. As the new face in town, NO ONE seemed friendly and while visiting the local corner store one day, someone said to me, "The kids say you are mean and I believe it!" (OMG…what do I do now? I had only been in the town less than a month!) I smiled and said that I am happy to be here and will surely try my best…It wasn't until a bit later before Christmas, this person found out that I liked to hunt game with my husband. I was OK then. I had made a connection. Hunting was a big deal within the community with a very active Rod and Gun Club. I made Outdoor Education a priority in my classroom.

So once you have listened, observed and been visible…and you have figured out what makes your community tick, then respect it and work with it! The situation is this: It is good to keep yourself neutral and some colleagues may disagree because you may feel you have a right to your opinion. For the most part you do, BUT You are the teacher of kids whose parents are at a mixture of political levels, a mixture of religions, and a mixture of beliefs that all may be different from your own.

Best advice…LISTEN and SMILE. Keep your personal, political and religious views to yourself.

The School District

Every school district is multi-layered. It takes a lot to educate the child, even though you, as teacher, are on the front line every day. Know your district from the inside out. That way, you will know if they walk the talk and mean what they say…and if they align with your vision.

What is the mission statement and future vision within your district? Do people really live it and believe it or are they pretty words that look nice on the school district wall and website. This is important to come to terms with because it may formulate where you fit in within the district, and ultimately determine how valued you feel…and your happiness.

The Situation could be this: A district claims that Respect is a Priority for All and Leadership is Shared at all pertinent levels. But then you discover later that your Great Idea for Literacy you developed with a colleague is welcomed at school but not supported or recognized at district level. The sharing ends there.

The School Board

A group of elected people come together to create district policy. Do they work together or are they argumentative? Do they support new ideas or do they point fingers? Do they listen or do they dictate? Go to Board Meetings if you can and find out. (I know you are busy in the classroom but see if you can make a few meetings…especially around Budget time.) Every teacher (and parent) should be aware of how funds come and go in your district.

The Big Leaders

The District Superintendent and Human Resources people are the Big Guns within each district that are instrumental in making sure the Mission and Vision statements are real. Your Spidey-sense will figure it out quickly…

Ray, was my favourite HR Guy in one district I worked in. He was also passionate about Curriculum Development. He was always visible and accessible. Ray encouraged teachers to share their knowledge and he always said that the Best Ideas came from Teachers, not the government gurus. I remember telling him that I was having a hard time finding resources on how to affectively teach fractions. He sent over a box of books; freebies he had picked up at conferences and each book was marked with sticky notes! Another time I asked him the same question around geometry. He said he'd come over and teach the first lesson. Wow! He was amazing and I taught that lesson the same way for 20 years. Thank you, Ray….

<u>Unions..</u>

If teachers in your part of the world are unionized, then life for you is quite different from those in an association.

For me, I started when administrators and teachers sat on the same side of the table. The Principal to me was the Principal Teacher in a school; the chief organizer and support when needed. I was lucky to have wonderful principals in my career. Association meetings were fun to go to; more of a social event than anything.

Then the world changed. Teachers wanted the option in contract to protest officially in strike form if necessary. The government, in turn, retaliated saying that if teachers wanted this, then they would join the Real World and become union and management. I was stunned! Suddenly my principal was now referred to as an AO, that is, an Administrative Officer. We now sat on opposite sides of the table. Truly an US vs THEM situation. It seemed that Education had adopted a factory mentality. How sad this day was…

I was one of the first people in a district to stand on a Picket Line. I was standing up for working and learning conditions and not a salary increase. I had old, low florescent lights in my classroom that gave me and some of my students' frequent headaches. I had documented this. The Board Office had full spectrum lighting but that was not for us. Hmmmmm Then I learned that we were not to have a salary increase but the Board gave themselves a healthy increase that year. Hmmmmmm.

Standing on a Picket Line in a Small Northern Town was not easy. The public came out to make sure we were not harassing their children who came to school and crossed the picket line. People I called good friends did not trust me and saw me as a trouble maker. It hurt because the Big Logging Company employees in town had just been on strike for 6 months, including over the summer and we helped most students prepare for the school year. That is, we gave kids our school supplies because families couldn't afford them. We also fed some of them too both breakfast and lunch! Hmmmm

I remember being quite emotionally upset over this and called my dad, who was a Big Pulp and Paper Executive. I grew up in a house of management. He told me to go to the beach and have a long talk with myself; specifically asking and answering the question, "Why do I want to be a teacher?"

I did this....yelling and screaming at the wind...I came back with the answer. "Because I like working with kids and I'm good at it...Because this action is what's best for kids..." My dad was understanding and encouraging. He said, "Then that is why you stand on that Picket Line...and smile confidently!"

And this is why You as a Teacher formulate your own Vision as I mentioned earlier. It drives you in times like this.

If you are unionized then go to the meetings and <u>Be Informed</u> of the Issues.

... .<u>But A Word of Caution Around Unions.</u> I was a unionized teacher from then on. But I observed a few Situations worth sharing along the way.

- Read and know your CONTRACT. Seriously. Know it and know your rights. BUT I learned that the CONTRACT is not the BE and END ALL. It is a GUIDE. It tries to account for every situation teachers will meet but, in reality, it can't. Situations come up and I will share a few with you where the contract was bent…Once against me and Once for me!

Situation #1. Living in a Small Town where the population was declining, there were to be several Board Forced Teacher Transfers to a neighbouring town within the district. The contract specifically said that, Seniority was not an issue in deciding who went but Necessary Qualifications were. I had just finished learning Braille and Mobility for a Visually Impaired student I was to get and suddenly I was told that I was to go…! In the guise of Management Fairness, 3 of us where forced to go and the Union made a deal with Management that Seniority was the only way to choose who would go. Not fair at all and I was choked!

Situation #2. In the long run, my transfer turned out to be a time where I experienced the Greatest Professional Learning and Personal Growth of my teaching career. So Someone was looking out for me. BUT one day, a year or so later, early in the school year, my Principal was not pleased that I had initiated a Grievance against her. I was stunned. I had NO idea what she was talking about…?!?!? Seems my Union Leader saw that I had a 15 minute weekly Prep time booked. I was entitled to 90 minutes a week and a minimum of 30 minutes at one time based on the Contract.

The Situation was this…I had a handicapped student that year, who came with an aide, but I wanted at least 30 minutes of uninterrupted time with this student each week by myself sooooo I decided to take 15 minutes of my prep time backed onto 15 minutes of recess time. My Principal supported my insistence on this idea, and as you can imagine, both of us were shocked at the grievance initiated by my Union Leader. There had been no discussion between myself and the Union Leader to clarify this. Again, I stood my ground around my Vision of Teaching. This action was what I knew to be best for the student I had. In the end the Union said OK to the idea. The Contract was Bent in my favour.

Watch out for Band Wagons. Be Informed, but fight the battles you feel are real and necessary. Soooooo many times I saw young new teachers jumping all over the hype at a Union Meeting, trying to impress the Old Guard of Teachers who had been in the district forever. And often it would be these Newbies who would stand up at the Board Meetings in protest of something obscure, that is, something I felt we could have talked over amicably with our Principals at a staff meeting. (One time I remember it was over how new curriculum was to be introduced. We could have solved that in house!) These Newbies were looking for validation from the Old Guard who smiled and sat back. Funny though, how these Newbies were often labelled as Trouble Makers, they had difficulty finding work away from our Small Northern Town. Learn from this as I saw it happen time and time again....

<u>Get involved with Professional Development.</u> If you have lots of time then be part of the PD committee. It is so satisfying to help each other in this way…AND it looks damn good on your resume.

Enough about unions…If you are lucky enough to be in an association, you are most likely to work amicably together and not get caught up in the union/management tussle. Enjoy.

<u>Support Staff</u>

You, as Teacher, are on the front line every day, but you can't do the job without Support Staff. These people include Maintenance, Custodians, Secretaries, Teacher Assistants, Aboriginal Support Workers, Home School Coordinators, etc.

Every one of these people is worth their weight in gold and I made an effort to get to know them. Some were cranky and some were cheerful but I always made the effort to validate and appreciate what they do. You may be the Big Gun with the Degree and they know it, but it does not hurt to say "Thanks so much for fixing that desk. That kid will be a lot more comfortable now." Or I'd give them something at Christmas. I let them know that we are ALL part of a Team that helps to educate the child. Everyone needs to feel valued. It always paid off.

The Maintenance and Grounds Crew are really special, hardworking people. I knew each by their first name and asked them all to call me as such. I knew a few who were miserable and cranky. A personal issue or a political one might be the reason for this but I would actively listen and stay neutral. Often people just need to be listened to. This is a valuable lesson I learned early, so take note. A smile and simple Thank You or an Appreciation DQ Ice Cream Cake goes a loooooong way...because when you have a blinking, florescent light in your classroom that drives you nuts or a leaky window where moisture wrecked a visual aid you liked...., you will appreciate maintenance!

Custodians are really important as they see the school from a totally different perspective. In cleaning up during late afternoon and evening hours, they see things you may not. Things like

-safety concerns. (The books on that shelve are not stable...or...the rebar sticking out of the pavement by the hopscotch.)

-casual observations around students or even staff. (Someone is peeing on the walls of the washroom in the primary ...or ..the waste basket in the hall....or a set of initials carved into school property...or..there are 'science experiments' in the staff fridge....)

I made sure my custodian was a part of the School Safety Committee. Their input was always valuable and appreciated. I remember one situation where we, as a staff, were concerned about a student who may be harboring thoughts of suicide. This child did see a counselor in and out of school...but one day our custodian found a crumpled up piece of paper outlining this child's Plan for suicide! I was called immediately as were all involved with this child. I was sooooo grateful for our custodian who, I know, felt a valuable part of our school team!

I often brought them dinner or a treat late at night...just to say thanks or listen to their thoughts.

Secretaries are truly the Hub of the Wheel at school. Their jobs have become more and more complex, specifically from a technological point of view. Appreciate what they do! Every Friday I stopped in at the local coffee shop and treated myself to one of the expensive milky things. At the same time I bought a treat for the Secretary. Just because…. She was always there to help me when the ^$*%^ hit the fan and I needed something Xeroxed fast or when a kid got sick or hurt or anytime I needed an extra adult in a discipline situation…. Blah Blah Blah.. Love your Secretary.

Teacher Assistants or Special Education Assistants as these people are referred to in my district, are trained and valuable beyond words. The best way to illustrate this is by example.

A Word about a Very Special Teacher Assistant;

Patricia Husberg.

Pat and I were a dynamic team for almost 8 years of my career. We liked each other. We respected each other and learned from each other as equals in helping to educate children. We even wrote down our experiential ideas for teaching Aboriginal culture and had a few lessons published during the Year of Indigenous Peoples, in a book called 500 Years and Beyond. This book might still be kicking around in some B.C. staffrooms.

I asked Pat to write down some things she thought were important for the Teacher-Teacher Assistant relationship to be successful…Here is her list…

-*A good TA should come in early, 5 to 10 minutes, to see what needs to be done. Talk to the teacher about the day.*

-*Watch the kids. Two sets of eyes are better than one and the teacher is always busy. Greet the kids. Note those whose manners are different, specifically if one has been crying. Mark it down in the Teacher's Day Book. Come up with a secret signal that 'something is amiss.'*

-*As a TA, have your own Day Book so the teacher can mark down something you need to know or prep for. It's also nice to have your own desk space and file drawer.*

-*Note hands that are up or kids that require attention. Go quietly. A one to one friendly face puts the child and ease, trusting you.*

-*Know the Class Rules. Be consistent and model them too.*

-*Make sure you are a part of a needy students Individual Education Plan meeting. Sometimes these will come in the form of regular school Team Meetings or IEP meetings around assessment time. If you are not invited then ask to be present. You spend time with that student, you should have a voice. These meetings may fall outside your regular hours of work. That's ok… Go anyway. Your dedication to kids will be noted.*

-*If the teacher is away a day, take notes in your book. The update via email or in their Day Book will be appreciated.*

-If you are a team player then use your intelligence and the training you were given. Offer to help set up a modified learning program for the teacher. Using the internet, old workbooks, old text resources or something from the District Resource Centre…Make up Learning Games. Board Games are easy to put together. Use your imagination…

You can also suggest simple crafts to keep fingers busy like spool knitting. It is fun and can align with Math, specifically the metric system. Crocheting or finger knitting is good too. If you just left these things in the back of a high school classroom, I bet they'd go for it, being the curious people they are.

-Expand your knowledge. Teachers do it so you should too. Take advantage of every Professional Development opportunity you can. It might not align with your union hours but do it anyway. It will speak well of how serious and conscientious you are about what you do.

So many parents came to us in the years ahead and said how much their children loved our classroom and asked what we did that made their kids like school. Well, it was simple. Pat and I saw each other as equals. We believed that every child could learn and we did it with patience, encouragement and respect. Kids trusted us.

If your school is lucky to have an Aboriginal Support Worker or Home School Coordinator then make sure you get to know these people well. I saw a few situations where these people were seen as bothersome when they entered a class. One colleague said to me, "It feels like they are watching me. I'm being judged." Well, don't be so defensive! I say, if you have another adult in the room, another pair of hands and eyes to help then EMBRACE IT! Thank them for coming in. If your Aboriginal Support Worker is there to help Aboriginal kids, GREAT! If he/she wants to teach something about aboriginal peoples, GREAT! Remember, aboriginal peoples were here before anyone else. The intelligence it took to live on the land in respect to the outdoor world is to be appreciated. More about Aboriginal learning later.....

Basically, the more people you have in your classroom, the better. They are good insurance. They can testify how you are with the kids if someone complains about you. You may never need to call upon it but it is nice to have. Love and respect all who enter your class. The Big People and the Little People. That is the Situation.

At Your School...

Wise words I ever heard from a senior teacher

. "If you really want know a school, talk to the person who has been there the longest."

So true. Once it was the custodian whom I got to know well because I spent a lot of time prepping for class late in the evening. Once it was, a teacher who helped me get to know the community. Once it was an Aboriginal Elder who had worked with the kids since the school opened. Again, she gave me wise words to this newbie as to how to fit in with the community. LISTEN!

- Principal.

    As an Elementary School Principal for 13 years I saw myself as a Servant. I had a sign above my door that said Principal Servant. I got lot of chuckles about that. "Hey, You the Head Slave around here?" ..Hahahaha ... My thinking was more like. "How can I help you do the job you need to do, Teacher, or Support Staff, or Parent or Child?"

Your Principal most likely had a hand in picking you for the school so you want to appreciate that and not disappoint. You have the good Work Ethic I talked about before and you listen. A Principal these days is not a Boss but more a Leader. Note the qualities of good leaders if you have aspirations of being one in the future. I did.

A good principal listens and supports you or gently guides you in the right direction. LISTEN if you are being asked to think about your work or actions. They have most likely sat in the hot seat at some point themselves. There were times I didn't always agree with my principal but I LISTENed and mulled the conversation over later. At one point I remember I was in charge of organizing a Pro D Event for the district. My principal liked to micromanage me sometimes so I went in (without any union representation) and diplomatically told him to trust me with the project. I would keep him informed but I didn't want him hovering about. After the event he told me he appreciated that little chat.

Also, another time, after talking to me about my handling of a student, the principal gently said," You can vent and say anything in my office, Sharlene. I can see you are quite stressed but remember outside to speak to the action, not the child." I never forgot that. That kid really tried my patience that day and I needed to say a few choice words. In reality, it was the actions that upset me even though at that point I was calling that child a few choicer words in my head. And in LISTENING to the bigger picture, I later came to understand why that student behaved annoyingly. It had nothing to do with me. I was the post. He needed love.

Follow The Protocol. AGAIN, I can't say enough about this. If you have a concern or a question, GO TO THE SOURCE! So many teachers or support staff are willing to yak behind backs or go online or run to the union rep before finding out the issue in its entirety. When teachers or parents came to me complaining, my first question was around did you talk to that person first before coming to me? Usually No. Soooooo many little issues can be cleared up with a diplomatic conversation. I will listen to the complaint but most school districts have and strictly enforce The Protocol. Here are a few Situations..

#1. Teacher to Teacher or Teacher Assistant. "Hey I heard you in the hallway today. You seemed upset. Are you ok now? Let me know how I can help. Next time you feel like that just send the student to my room for a time out."

#2 Teacher to Parent " Glad you came in and told me how Mary is feeling being in my room. Can we talk to her together and come up with a solution? She doesn't like it when I ask her to be quiet when I am giving instructions. She is feeling picked on. Can we agree what her job is and what mine is? What is a visual cue we could use?

#3 Teacher to Student "Johnny, I heard you out on the playground today complaining about me having to keep you in at recess. I want to talk to you about this and let you know that recess was the only time we had to work on your math today. I didn't want you to go home and worry about those last few problems you need to finish. Call me later if you need more help, ok?"

Now there are a million Situations I could list here and you will too after some teaching experience. The Protocol being said, there are some Situations where it not be followed, specifically if you suspect serious abuse of a child, or a colleague in distress (i.e. an emotional breakdown, drinking etc....). This is Common Sense....right?

Enough said...

<u>A final note about Your Principal</u>... This person will most likely be called if you are seeking employment elsewhere. In fairness to teachers, most districts have a set of interview and reference questions that are the same for all. BUT there is one little question we all ask and you should know this.....

"If you had the opportunity to hire or keep... (Your Name) at your school, would you?"

Hmmm, now you think about this. If the answer is Yes! Followed by Blah Blah Blah, extolling your virtues, it will most likely be because of your Work Ethic, Your extra effort with kids, Your Honesty in Good and Bad Situations and You Really are a Team Player.

If No..well then usually no more is asked and no more is said ...other than the basic district questions.

- <u>Teacher Types</u>

  You, being the hard working, putting-kids-first, good working ethic, going the extra mile, caring, enthusiastic Teacher that you are, will be surprised to find others that are not.

  The Public is often quite free with labeling us as That Good Teacher, That Bad One….and we sometimes see it in our colleagues. It is sad to see but in fairness to Teachers everywhere, You are human, even though the Public expects you to be nothing short of Perfect.

  Saying that, the Situation is this. I have known colleagues who

  -were just hanging in there until retirement, counting the days.

  -were so politically minded to the point that it drives everything in their world. They are always hard done by. Never happy.

  -were Star Teachers …..with very Sharp Points.

  -were so upset over a failed relationship, their anger shows up at school.

  -were single parents trying to cope.

  -were bullies.

  -were jealous of the success of others.

-were always resistant to change. They have taught this way for Blah Blah years. It was good then so it is good now.

-were afraid to try something new whether it was technology or curriculum.

-were always blaming parents.

-always felt the need to dominate the Staff Meeting.

-lived on the laurels of their past and never moved forward.

I could psychoanalyze the 'why' of each one here but I won't. And you may be able to read between the lines here on some of the above teacher types. The reality is, that all teachers are not the same. It can be thrilling and also disappointing. You may be able to help some of them in big and little ways, but others don't budge. Stand tall, don't be intimidated or bullied. You worked too hard to get where you are. Speak diplomatically not emotionally.

So..what do you do??

• YOU go back to that Belief Statement you put together when you first became a teacher. I talked about this earlier and I keep coming back to it! You stick those words on your fridge, on your bathroom mirror and on your desk! You may not be able to fix the adult problems of the world but for 10 months you can made a difference in the life of children.

- Embrace change. The best thing about Education is that it consistently evolves. Sheesh..We've come from Overheads to Document Cameras, from blackboards to whiteboards to Smart Boards. There is always something new!

  There is always new research around learning, how the brain works, what works, what doesn't, best practices etc. Stuff like this makes great summer reading. I had an awesome Assistant Superintendent and an HR person who would send us new books or short, 1-2 page articles that sparked thinking. I always didn't have time to read everything but I kept these articles in a folder by my chair at home. I would digest them when I had time. Quiet time, with a glass of red wine time. I didn't always agree with everything new. I remember when I saw math and reading curriculum changes come around in circles. They just had different catch titles. For example, Individualized Reading became Whole Language. That was ok. Change sparked conversation among colleagues and that was a Situation I liked!

- Learn from those Teachers who are Great! I was so blessed to have experienced Great teachers when I first started out. I still remember them fondly. They smiled every day. They embraced changed. Simply, they loved kids and kids loved them. They fired me with energy and picked me up when I needed a hand.

  Specifically, I remember one day when I was teaching a Grade 4-5 class. I had 7 kids with specific needs and minimal help. I was down and didn't feel like I was making headway...

A very special colleague who had a class much like mine, listened to me Whaaa Whaaa Whaaa and then said, "Yes, but Sharlene, what other profession is there where you really get to make a difference in the lives of people. I wouldn't want to do anything else." OMG, I did an about-face and NEVER forgot that.

AND, my final words for this section are that you will find more teachers like this in Education. Teachers are truly a dedicated group of people. They are not there for the money and they will spend a big chunk of their summers upgrading. I know and really believe that the Great Ones faaaaaar outweigh the Others.

The Best Ideas for the Classroom come from those who are in it every day! These teachers' Ideas should be embraced and shared and I would hope that they see this at the management level of school districts. I have seen teachers create curriculum and assessments that work. A little encouragement and support to teachers in Big and Little Ways helps to make Great Teachers even Greater.

• The Parents

The Difference between Now and Then...When I started teaching in the 70's, parents supported me as I moved through 3 school districts and you always felt their support as we worked together.....BUT now it is a different story. Parents seem to view school with a lot of mistrust and the reasons are a mixed bag...

What happened? Simple answer is; Families Changed. Post war Canada had more moms at home. Mine was, all through my growing up years. Dads worked. Now with changes within our economy, families need 2 parents working. I only stayed home for a few years when my kids were young and then I went back to work. Two incomes are needed to make that mortgage payment, food, bills and have some leftover for holidays and treats. In later years I saw more working moms, more working single parents, more split homes, more dysfunctional homes and more blended families. Parenting is stressful and it is work. ....so

DON'T criticize parents! The Situation is this. They will make you laugh, make you cry, hurt your feelings, compliment you, yell at you, talk about you on line or in the parking lot, they will smile when they see you or ignore you.....Still, DON'T criticize them. Why?

Because, a wise educator told me, "Parents are doing the best they can with what they know."

Think about it. No one gets advance training for parenting. You wing it based on how you were raised or what you learn from others. Parenting is the hardest job of all. Some of my students would tell me that their moms don't do anything. They just stay at home. So I would explain to them about parenting being the 24-Hour-No-Days-Off Job. That is why I feel teacher training programs should include some child care.

Parents come to you with their own experiences from school. Some good, some not. Parents may come from dysfunctional homes, split homes, blended families, and single parents. Parents may be intimidated because of your years at university. Parents can be offended if you criticize their kids as they may see it as a reflection or criticism of them.

I have talked about making a connection with parents in Chapter Three. Go back now and skim through it.

Empower parents. Show them your plan for the year. If they don't come to the class meeting, sent an info sheet home. Have them call you by your first name. Give them your school email and home phone number because if there is a crisis, you want to know as soon as possible and not when you arrive in the morning. Invite them to help at school or on field trips. Have kids write what they learned each day in an agenda book and ask parents to sign it.

I would always tell my parents that if there is stress at home for any reason, either call me OR a signature or initials on unfinished work, gave me a heads up that something was amiss. I did not need to know the specifics. Our homes and marriages are not always perfect, eh? I made sure I got to that kid the next day. To help them, not to pepper them with questions about home.

I always tried to get the message to parents that we are Partners not Adversaries.

Let parents know you support them..or ask how you can help or support them. This message is comforting to most. It might be as simple as homework help, or help with lunch.

And no matter how wonderful you are, you may meet parents who will just not like you for one reason or another. You feel they don't trust you and you are always criticized. This is why I ask teacher training programs to teach conflict resolution. You are in the public eye and often you will feel like the bug or the windshield. Make sure you share the situation with your principal and colleagues. Reread and hang on to that Believe Statement you made when you started. I told my teachers that it was my job to shield them from this, especially if verbal abuse happens at school. Say.."Let's take this concern to the office." Come to me and talk to me. It is most often not a reflection of your teaching or you personally. My teachers knew I had their back.

As a principal I had many parents enter my office angry and ready to 'shake down the little lady'. Hmmm I sat. I listened respectfully without interruption. I paraphrased the concern. I kept my voice quiet. Away from the eyes of others, the issues often had NOTHING to do with school. It was the job, no money, bad marriage, legal troubles etc.....People needing help. These conversations sometimes ended up with tears. ...and all I did was listen. I could point them in the direction of the Food Bank, Social Services, Family Services and that is where your Home School Coordinators are valuable if you are lucky to have them.

A quick reflection here. I had a parent years ago who was so angry with me over a misinterpretation;

something that I felt could be cleared up with a conversation. She started a campaign to malign me with letters to my principal, the Parent Advisory Council, The Board Office and then letters to my fellow teachers… With the help and support of my principal, I wrote her back but she never came to the table to talk. Eventually this wore me down emotionally and I felt on the edge when the Superintendent came to talk to me. Of course, I broke down weeping as he sat listening to me grinning!?!?! Then he said, "Well, Sharlene, when you are dealing with Wing Nuts, it is a No Win Situation!" I snapped out of it quickly as his somewhat abrupt message to me was simply that I will not please everyone. Lesson Learned and never forgotten!

Do Not Beat yourself up over mistakes made…OR dwell on that difficult parent. I know that is easier said than done, but you are NOT perfect. You are human and you cannot fix the entire world. As a Broken Record….. Gently let that parent know, you are doing your best and you are here to support them, You are doing your best and you are here to support them……

No need to tell you about the confidentiality thing here, right?? You keep all you know about families and their children at the school.

Wine was invented for trying times like these…

The ABC Rule – Parents or the general public, that see you outside the school will often ask you about your day, especially if you looked a little haggard in the grocery store. NEVER admit to a bad day with the public. Remember that they are paying you a good wage today to be with their children. They expect and deserve the best from you. They do not want to hear that you did not have a good day! I would smile and say, "O it is Always Busy and Challenging."...my ABC rule. Now, if you need to vent, do it with your principal or colleagues. Keep it at school. ..Or if you have a wonderful spouse like I do, consider yourself damn lucky.

<u>Ps</u>. Put your feet up. Have some wine. Tomorrow is another day.

More often than not, your parents will appreciate you but they may never tell you...until one day, you will get a phone call out of the blue. It is a parent from year's back who wants to let you know that their child is graduating and their son says that you were one of his favourite teachers. And that is why you do what you do!

- The Kids

In writing this book, I got hung up at this point because this chat about kids could be a book in itself! The topic is too big and so I have tried to narrow it down, giving the reader the Important Situations I think you should know...

- The Education Situation.

Kids are like a mixed bag of gourmet jelly beans. Each one different and each one is special. And even though you may have many years of teaching under your belt, one child will come along and set all your sweet little strategies on its ear! This happened to me right to the last year. It is a humbling experience but always good to know that one model of teaching does not fit all. It's like people feeling how lucky they are to have their kids in a single grade room and not a grade split. Huh?? Do all six year olds learn at the same rate? Obviously no.

Another way of thinking about this is to imagine 2 kids entering Kindergarten. One has been read to from the womb and the other has rarely seen a book since birth. Do these two kids learn at the same rate? Will they be on the same academic level at Grade 6? Maybe…but so many factors depend on their learning from here to there.

It is such a thrill to see a student who has been struggling suddenly catch fire and academically take off! I still play some of these memorable moments over and over in my head, like an old movie. You don't forget them…

•   Multi-Sensory Teaching

"If a child can't learn the way we teach, maybe we should teach the way they learn." *(Ignacio Estrada)*

This is good to keep in mind because kids learn in so many different ways. Some are more visual, some more auditory, and some kinesthetic. Most are a combination of these and that is why Multi-Sensory Teaching was my favourite teaching style. It works. Kids learn and retain information if you can incorporate it visually, auditorily and add some movement. I would do this from K to Grade 12. Minimize the lecturing, the sage on the stage if you can. I invented individual and whole class games to help kids learn things like the times tables. I kept beanbags and small balls in my class for this. I took kids outside with skipping ropes to learn spelling words and they could recite them frontwards and backwards.

Multi-sensory Teaching is why computer learning is so successful! It incorporates the visual, auditory senses and it is tactile. Computers reward successes with a Yahoo and they are also quiet and patient…waiting for the answer.

Capitalize on their interests if you know it or find it. I had a student enjoy our dinosaur unit. I used that spark of interest in every other subject. I put dinos on his math work. I bought dino stickers..blah blah…you get the idea. Same for a kid I had in Grade 8 Science who loved Rockets… Well, being a space trekky myself, I filled his cup with all the space knowledge I knew. I'd leave him with something like, "Hey Marty. Have you heard about the Hadron Collider and the Higgs Boson? Google it! It's cool stuff." This led to us sharing knowledge and it was great how the rest of his academics improved. He may turn out to be a leading astronomer one day.….

- Make Learning Relevant.

This is easier said than done because kids want to know why they have to learn this or that. For the most part, when it came to something they had no interest in and you are bound by the curriculum, I would say something like …"I would like to talk to you on an adult level when I say that this subject is needed for your general knowledge of the world."

-If it is Social Studies or History I'd add "Learning about our Past can help us to make the Future better and You are going to a place in Time I will not see. I need you to make the Future a good one for my Grandchildren."

I could usually manage this conversation around other subject areas too like Science, Math, Language Arts……

I shared some traveling photos with my kids. Some from Mexico, some from Europe, some from the Orient. I said that I was glad I could use the little French I learned in school to understand a map or read a menu in Europe. Also it was nice to have a meaningful conversation with other people who had visited Stonehenge in England or Anne Frank's house in Amsterdam or Peace Park in Hiroshima or walked on the Great Wall of China.

Talking to them respectfully on a mature level, acknowledging the fact that they are the one species on the planet capable of intelligent thinking and letting them know We want the Best for our Future is usually a good argument. They may not buy it then but kids will think about what you said, IF you are sincere. Kids have a sure fire BS Meter if you are not!

Teach Kids to Think! Often so much of teaching is regurgitation. We are running to fit the curriculum into 10 months. Remember those Profs you learned from in university; those good ones we mentioned before that allowed you to think and write your thoughts on their subject. After you present the basic concepts of any unit, take the time to engage students into thinking about what they have learned. I saw the importance of this early on. I remember having our District Resource Center bring in a great Thinking Kit I saw at a conference. It was brilliant and I also noticed that I was only one of a few teachers to request it every year. Kids are naturally curious and love to ask 'Why?'. So initiate debates around novel study characters, social studies what-if questions, science present and future issues. I loved to present a question on the board at the beginning of a lesson and have them write their final thoughts around it as their ticket out the door.

Allowing and promoting Critical Thinking is great for all learning levels. The quick kids can expand their knowledge and thinking through media research. The slower ones can build or draw. I remember a student in Grade 4 with a severe reading/writing disability who could build anything. His parents encouraged this and he was putting together mechanized Lego creations before they came on the market. He turned out to be a Heavy Duty mechanic and makes more $$ than I ever did. School and home, working together. Amazing, eh?

<u>Character Education</u>. It was the necessity of teaching the importance of having a good Character that really surprised me in my later years. These were things taught more at home and complimented at church years ago…..Not so much now it seems…

Teaching the relevance and the importance of saying Please, Thank You, and Excuse Me was a part of every school year. Good manners do not cost anything and good manners go a long way. A good mannered person gets hired in the workplace. You, as teacher, model it and live it. Some examples…

• I told my students a story about our son when he was 2 years old. We took him to a restaurant for fish and chips. The restaurant was really busy with only one waitress. It was loud. We ordered. She brought a large order for our son forgetting that we had asked for a kid's portion. When he saw it, he stood up on his chair, looked at her said, "THAAAANK YOU, Ma'am!!!" The restaurant went quiet and she said, "Young Sir, that is the first Thank You I have heard today. Your meal is free!" Hmmmm, a 2 year old teaches others about manners.

This story generated such good conversations with kids and their experiences around manners and rudeness they remember. I would tell them that my Grandmother told me that "When people are being rude and hurtful, that is when they need Loving or Kindness the most." This was a brainful for a young teen like me But I NEVER forgot it.

I also led a Leadership Club at school. I told them Leadership is not being the boss, it is serving and empowering others. We did things like make Christmas Cards for Seniors and then sing for them. Or we shoveled driveways....just because it was a good thing to do. When they see appreciation from doing the right thing because it's the right thing to do, kids see the relevance of good manners... It sticks.

Other good character lessons are around the importance of Honesty, Perseverance, Patience, Integrity, Being Positive, Kindness...and Paying a Kindness Forward. So many good lessons around these and others can be found on line. It just takes a 15 minute conversation with kids a few times a week to help them understand that having a GOOD Character will help them succeed and it is what employers want. Employers are looking for team players with good interpersonal skills. Bring a Business CEO or Executive in and ask them! Also ask this company executive about resumes and applications (thus, reinforcing why they need to write neatly, spell or write coherently). Ask them about the Interview Process, thus reinforcing why kids need to speak well...

Kids will get the relevance of this. I remember reviewing Perseverance with a group of kids and using Terry Fox and Helen Keller as examples. A few years later, a student told me that because of that lesson, he was able to overcome his home life and move on successfully....

sniff Enough said....

Classroom Management/Discipline/Bullying

The Situation is this: No matter how full your Tool Box is around this and no matter how many teaching years you have under your belt, there will be days and times when you feel like you just don't have it all together.

The best rule of thumb here is <u>Prevention</u>...setting the stage, outlining your expectations and being consistent. Even as a Teacher On Call, where you don't know the class or how it runs, generally you can set a Goal for the Day with the class, go outside and play some games for 15 minutes and then come in and start the day. Usually this sets the mood and tone collectively. Your Day Goal can be as simple as Be Kind Today.

Note that here I mentioned to do something physical at the beginning of the day. This does work and the reasoning being that kids come to school from all directions and in a variety of emotional states every day. Just like parents can tell what kind of a day their child had at school, YOU can tell how parents send them. If you take 15 minutes right after attendance to take the kids for a whole class physical activity such as outside skipping, four square, basketball...anything that works. I did this in all kinds of weather. At one school I worked at, I found a covered area where maintenance kept equipment. For the most part, this brings all the kids together at a common emotional level before you get into the days academics. I would even do this for high school kids. I knew a high school teacher who would do 10 minutes of yoga and breathing with his class before starting the day. At first the kids thought Mr. D was flakey but they all sure liked his class!

Singing for 10 to 15 minutes works too. You can play anything on the guitar using the C, G and D7 chords, but if you don't play an instrument you can download anything fun and even put up the words and use the Karaoke version of the song. When that song, "Happy" by Pharrell Williams came out, I heard it everywhere! It just put a skip in everyone's step.

AND be sure to stand up and Welcome your Kids to class every day! I stood by the door and greeted them. This way I could gauge their moods. Even the troubled kids will appreciate this though you may think they don't. Kids who are troubled like routine and will wonder why you weren't at the door that day…. I remember the year I retired. I met the kids daily and I always did the Friday Happy Dance for the kids coming off the bus. The older kids laughed at me and thought I was weird…but one of them said to me, "When you go, who is going to do the Friday Happy Dance?" I told her she needed to teach the next Principal to do it.

Kids notice things…Kids notice everything you do and everything you say along with everything you wear. I liked to wear geeky jewelry that celebrated every seasonal occasion. I had a collection. Others I know wore crazy socks or ties...

If you are the Teacher, you know to have the Class Contract set with the students the first week of school. This is a process where we all know how to get along. You also know to post it close to the board for all to see. (..and send it home too. I did this and families used it as a Home Contract having family meetings around dinner time where issues could be voiced and resolved.)

The Best Practice I ever found was Restitution: Restructuring School Discipline by Diane Chelsom Gossen (1996). Its philosophy is around doing what is right because it is the right thing to do. This follows most Aboriginal teachings as well. Diane is a Canadian from the Prairies and her workshops are worth going to. Her resources for teachers are cheap and worth getting. Diane talks about the basic needs of kids, how and why they act out. The Restitution Model works better than the Reward and Punishment, Carrot and Stick Approach...AND if you do some Character Education with it, you will be well on your way to feeling like you're on top of your game. As Principal, here is a typical conversation I might have with a troubled student sent to the office....

P: Hi Come on in...what's up? (Gauging the student, I often took conversations out of the office. We'd go to the kitchen for something to eat, or outside for a Walk and Talk.)

S: I'm in trouble. I got mad and swore.

P: What's your plan to make this right?

S: I dunno

P: If you did know, what would it look like?

S: You're gonna do what you want to me anyway?

P: So you want Me to be in control of You....or do You want to be in control of You?

S: Huh?

P: *(I repeat what I said. If the kid is sassy and rude, then they want me to be in control and I may suggest some restitution activity after an apology is heard.)*

S: I want to be in control of me and I guess I could say sorry.

P: Sorry is a good way to start..but what is your plan to make this right and ensure it doesn't happen again? *(Sorry is always the best start but it doesn't let the behavior off the hook. The behaviour comes with a consequence for the action... hopefully something they have decided and not me. Sometimes a little coaching helps with a few possible suggestions.)*

S: I'll apologize and I'll tell my teacher that I will wash the desks after lunch for a week. I'll also write a paragraph about why it isn't a good idea to swear and read it to the younger classes. *(Kids are usually harder on themselves and a natural consequence like the students second suggestion is better than desk washing.)*

But there are those kids who are so troubled, they have a hard time finding ways to help themselves.

They can be in survival mode. I found these kids usually came with Emotional Issues and they are often the hardest to reach or teach. These kids were often dealing with things I couldn't imagine around abuse or neglect. Their behaviours needed to be addressed but with empathy and love.

I remember, as a teacher, telling one young man who was violent the first day of school, "I may not make a difference in your life this year but I will Never hit you and I will Never yell at you. Every time I need to send you to the office I will look at you with these eyes and I am telling you that I Care about You and I Believe in the Good Person you are Inside. Never Forget this." I only had one or two more violent incidents with this young man where as other teachers before me had a year full of them. This young man was dealing with a lot in his personal life and just needed love.

There are those with special needs who don't fit this model and you will need the help of the Special Ed team to create a Behaviour Plan that all can work with. You will need to administer a consequence but do it with love.

You get the idea? It's like Restorative Justice. The person faces their problem and solves it, hopefully for themselves. And it's nice to be able to tell parents that their child did have trouble in school today and came up with a plan to correct it.

Bullying is a huge problem even though it's been around forever. More so now perhaps because the act of bullying has carried into cyberspace, belittling others in horrible ways. There are a lot of good programs out there but the one I found that worked best for my elementary school was the W.I.T.S. Program put out by the Rock Solid Foundation in Victoria, BC. It was started by the Victoria City Police who were shocked at the death of a young high school student killed by her peers. She was bullied and accused of looking at someone's boyfriend. The kids killed her under a bridge. When questioned by police, the kids were more concerned about who had ratted them out rather than the act of murder. The police were shocked by this realization and felt that kids needed to TELL someone when they were being bullied, even if they needed to tell over and over again and tell someone they could trust. The acronym they designed was to use your WITS when you are feeling bullied.

W = Walk Away but tell and adult

I = Ignore the Behaviour but tell and adult

T = Talk it Out but tell and adult

S = Stay calm, Seek help. Tell an adult

Every student in our school knew this from Kindergarten to Grade 7. It was in our student agenda and posted in several places within the school.

Putting Restitution and the WITS Program together, kids would come to my office a lot less and when they did, the first thing they would say was. "OOKOKOK I Forgot to use my WITS and my plan to make it right is......."

As for high school, I think the Rock Solid Group would come to your school. ...and I know several high schools that use Restorative Justice Teams consisting of an Administrator, an Aboriginal Elder, a Teacher, a member of your Parent Group ... as a means for discipline and it works! It is more time consuming but more effective.

There are sooooooo many programs and ideas out there that work. These ones were mine. If you find something tried and true, TALK about it. Share it with others...

- <u>Children with Special Needs</u>

Children with Special Needs are just that, Special. These kids usually generate support funding and the process to get it is often long and stressful. Specific testing, interviews with parents, more testing, class juggling, and teacher juggling...Finding the best fit for this child is really a task and priority for all.

In my career, I learned Braille and Mobility for a Visually Impaired student, I learned some Deaf Sign too for another, and I learned how to deal with epilepsy, cerebral palsy and petit mal seizures. More and more I found that these kids deserved to be in the school system and they deserved inclusive education (Not stuck in the Odd Class Mixture at the end of the hall) and they deserved to see themselves as learners. One school I came in contact with when transferring a student needed to know the specific IQ for the child and told me she would be enrolled in their Opportunity Class. I said NO (!!!).... with support she could cope quite well in a regular class. The school did not listen and I felt that all the work we had done to help this child envision herself as a Learner was going to go down the drain. She moved but returned to our school system within 2 years. She has learning disabilities but with the great support she has received, she is thriving and will be a productive citizen of the world.

Thank God for computers because the brilliance of new technology is a Real Connection to the world for these kids whether it is a Picture-Symbol Board, a Talking Laptop, a Record and Talk Module, an Ipad loaded with learning apps....Whatever!

Most teachers receive a minimal amount of training around kids with learning disabilities and special needs, specifically, dealing with dyslexia or ADD or ADHD and perhaps a little knowledge around Fetal Alcohol Syndrome. Teachers who have dealt with kids with Special Needs in their practicums are really ahead of the game here...why? Because you will have observed and come to know that kids with Special Needs are the real Teachers. They teach everyone in their World about the Diversity of Life, about Tolerance, about Patience, about Perseverance and about Being Grateful for the Life each of us is given.

So, the Situation is this. Mr. and Mrs. Johnson want to put their child with Special Needs into your school, your class. What do you do? In thinking about this section of the book, I realized that We with our Big Degrees in Education are Not the experts. I asked two sets of parents to help me here. They are the most courageous parents I have ever known. They both have had a child with Special Needs in the school system, and not with common disabilities. They are waaaaay off the grid! Take the time to Google each disability. I asked these two sets of parents the question: What do Teachers Need to Know? Here are their stories....

Nathan with Sanfilippo Syndrome Type A

Parents: Jean and Nels

Nathan loved school and the friends he made he had for life. The scariest moment for us was when we left our son in the care of people we did not know. There were good times with the school system and times we were unhappy with each other.

Before Nathan started Kindergarten, my husband and I went and interviewed schools to find the right fit for us as a family. We talked to three schools and we designed a list of specific questions beforehand. And because Nathan had a rare syndrome, we brought information for them to read and left it at the school. We even sent an Information Package for the school prior to our interview.

We believed that every child has the right to go to public school. Our child did not learn to read or write. He was there for social interaction with his peers and visual academic sparks and stimulation where it could be found. I worked with the teachers in finding ways that we as a family could get the kids involved in Nathans life.

When Nathan started Kindergarten I came up with a plan to help the teacher and the class understand Nathan. He had a wheel chair then for when his legs got sore. Most children at that age had never seen a wheel chair or envisioned them as part of people who were sick or old. Because Nathans Syndrome was too hard for younger children to understand, I kept it very simple. I put Nathan in his chair in the middle of a circle of students. I had the kids walk around the chair. I encouraged them to tell me what they saw and to touch the chair or Nathan. Most of the children were a little apprehensive at first but they soon realized there was nothing to be afraid of. I also wrote a letter to the parents telling them about our son and what he had; also inviting their phone calls if they had any questions for us and we directed them to an informational website. The teacher was so impressed with this Show and Tell experience, I was asked to do this for all the elementary classes as an introduction of our son to the school world.

I remember Nathans Grade 5 class was learning about their community. They wrote about their homes and neighbourhood. As Nathan was unable to talk, we used a large round recording devise. We called it the Big Button. I recorded my voice into Nathans Big Button telling the children about his home and family. Children in his class took turns each week pressing the button, listening to what they heard, writing what they heard and drawing pictures. This helped his class with listening and writing skills. At the end of the year, the class compiled these writings and pictures into a book Nathan took home. What a lovely souvenir of his Grade 5 year. The Big Button was used for so many things throughout his years at this school. Nathan was an accepted part of school.

As Nathan got older, he was wheelchair bound and had a feeding tube. He went to Grade 7 where there were 20-25 kids in the class. I suggested a Bulletin Board be set up for Nathan. I was able to get the children of the school involved in fundraising for awareness around Sanfilippo Syndrome. When Nathan needed a new wheelchair, we had the entire school involved in picking the colour. Two choices dominated and the kids voted ORANGE as the winner!

We, as parents, made sure the school was aware of any medical changes that could impact Nathans life at school. We helped the school come up with a plan that needed to be in place for the next level of his development. When we had a teacher come up with reasons as to why Nathan could not do certain things in the classroom, like play on the computer as he drooled a lot, we offered to get a cover for the keyboard. We tried to find solutions to the problems that would come up.

I would specifically tell teachers that the parent knows their child the best; listen to them first. They have to deal with something most of you will never have to deal with.

Nathan was given 10 to 12 years to live. He lived to be 13. We were very blessed with this. I am very pleased with the time he had at school.

<u>My final thoughts around Nathan</u>. This young man had quality of life. These two amazing parents, and grandmother, made sure he was involved in everything he could be a part of. Nathan went to Disney World and another time he met his favourite NHL hockey player. Knowing that this child would not live long, I rarely ever saw this family without a smile or positive outlook. Jean was acknowledged by her city council for being an advocate for her work with children with Special Needs. She and her husband, as well as Nathans grandmother, still provide respite care to others today.

Brian with Williams Syndrome

Parents: Tom and Darla

DON'T LIE TO ME.

ASK ME.

I AM HERE TO HELP YOU.

WE NEED TO WORK AS A TEAM.

I am the parent of a developmentally delayed adult. School was not a happy place for him. This is our story:

Background:

Our son is the third of four children (less than 5 years between them all). We knew what he should be doing by the others examples. It took 3 ½ years to get a "label". My husband and I sat on one side of a conference table and a half a dozen doctors on the other. We were told our son would not be a productive member of society, not be able to learn or live on his own and we should consider putting him in an institution. We chose not to listen. (None of these came true!)

Elementary School:

Our son had been assessed by the school, met the future teacher and she had specialized equipment ready for him. We were all excited. BUT, at 9:30 PM the night before he was to start school (and ride the bus like the big kids) we got a call telling us they had too many kids in that class and had to sort it out. Try telling your child the next morning after he helped pack his lunch, pick the clothes he would wear for the big day that he wasn't going now! It took several weeks for them to invent another class of all special needs kids in another school. The following year the exact same scenario played out!

We had asked for our boy to attend our local school for the half days he wasn't at the special class. No was the reply. So, after networking with other parents in the same boat, they had made appointments with the school district superintendent. The earliest, 3 months later!

I thought this was unacceptable so I walked into the district office, and walked to his office and asked him for 5 minutes of his time. I told him my request and said I didn't want a teacher's aide with him during that time as he was only in Kindergarten and he wasn't a behaviour problem. The Super said yes, and then the teacher in our "home school" wasn't willing to have him in her class. After I said I would be there to support her, and come get him at a moment's notice she agreed, and voila he was in. He was the first special needs child she had taught and later said it was the best experience of her career.

At the same time we were networking with families that had the same "label" as our child. They told us these kids learned to write by a combination of printing and writing where the child's hand does not leave the paper. It made sense to me. But, the teachers in elementary school didn't agree and refused to try it. (I asked every year). So my son did not learn to write except for a sketchy printing of his name.

By grade 3 and 4 he was genuinely interested in some subjects and so I asked the teacher to give me maybe 5 out of the 20 facts she wanted him to learn in each subject. I wrote "bedtime stories" incorporating all these facts and read to him every night. It was amazing how much he learned! Sadly, I couldn't keep this up after I started working full time and was busy with our other children. I asked if the teachers' aid could write them for me. I got a big NO for an answer again.

At the same time he was once again assessed as needing a computer to do his school work. (There was one pegged for him in his first school placement, before he got bumped out of that class.) We were promised every year that he would get one and then when September rolled around we were told there wasn't room in the budget but next year for sure. Next year never came so we purchased a laptop ourselves, loaded it with the programs they requested, put a laminated, typed memo of how to turn it on, save files, and turn it off on the outside as computers were not so common then. We were assured by the teacher that they were using it and it was a wonderful tool. We found out at the end of that year we were lied to once again and they had not used the resource as nobody knew how to use it. The instructions were specific and if they had asked, I would have taken time off work to show them how to use it.

During his elementary years we relocated to another school district. They told us YES we integrate special needs students here and they were excited about him coming. Well guess what: they lied to us. He was the first one.

High school:

Oh where to begin??? You know that classroom behind the principal's office? Well that's where my son spent most of his time between grade 7 and 12. He was bullied every year and every year came home with a black eye. It happened in this class behind the office. This class had one teacher, 4 or 5 teacher aids and most years around 8-12 students. With multiple discussions with the teacher responsible I asked multiple times to not pair my son with the child that kept hurting him. They said "of course not." Well you guessed it, they lied to me. One of the worse things to happen was this same "bully" sprayed hot glue from a glue gun on both of my son's hands, front and back the day before Christmas break. My first question was "why are they using HOT glue guns in a special needs class?"

As parents we were still networking with other families that had the same "label". At one such encounter we were told about a wonderful reading program that many of our children were successful at learning to read with. So I head back to the school and enquire if they have said program. They lied to me and said they had never heard of it. I came with an order form and told them where they can get it. Miraculously they produced their own catalogue with this program in it. When I asked if they could order it in May so that it would be there to start in September the following year, I was told no, there is no room in the budget and they will wait till September to order it. I suggested I would pay for it as if they order it in September it won't arrive till December. After much "negotiations" they ordered it. Well September comes and I enquire if they are using this reading program and I am assured that yes they are and they are pleased with his progress. I asked about 4 months in a row how it was going and always got that same answer. Then out of the blue, one of the teacher aids told me that in fact they were not using that program and never had because when they ordered it, the workbook that came with it did not belong to the reader. You guessed it, the teacher had been lying to me for months. Sadly, for whatever reason, our son did not learn to read beyond a mid-grade one level.

Another scenario that was unacceptable and totally frustrating was when we asked if our son could be in a grade 9 science class. He had a keen interest and we thought a couple more hours away from "that room behind the office" would be good for him too. Well, it didn't go over very well as we were told he didn't complete science 8 so how could he possible go in the next class? Well he wasn't going to graduate with a high school diploma. (He had a special needs diploma at the end). Again with much discussion we were happy to be told that yes, he can attend that class. We were ecstatic! Happy that is until we found out a few weeks later, that yes, our son was attending grade 9 science: But so were 5 others from that class behind the office escorted by one teacher's aide. I know for a fact that none of those other kids' parents went in and asked for that.

For several years our son was put into an "anger management" class. He never had behavioural or anger issues. He is prone to "the power of suggestion" so we fought every year to not have him go to that class. But every year they put him in it. I understand they need to have a minimum number of students to conduct it, but to us it was just a time filler that could have been spent more productive for him.

A teachers' aid went to shop class with a group of these "labelled" kids and became very proficient at "shop" because the kids were not allowed to use the tools. Our son used power tools and an air compressor at home with the proper personal protective equipment. He learned nothing in that class. And they never listened to me when I told them he was capable.

We briefed the teachers every year on our son's medical conditions and what to look for. I get it that you can't remember all that when you have a few dozen kids in some classes. BUT when a sibling comes into the classroom and says her brother needs to go to the hospital immediately please listen and take him. She knows! (The teacher refused in this case and the aid, grabbed her car keys, and took our son and sibling.) I can't thank the aid or the sibling enough for that day.

These were just a sampling of stories we could tell you from our son's time in the school system. There are so many more! When our son finished grade 12 we were told he could stay a couple more years, till he was 20 or 21? We declined. We were all done! Now I sound like I am that mom from hell who demands and yells at the classroom teacher, but I never was. I never raised my voice. I was always supportive and available to help with fieldtrips or any other role needed by parents. I did this for all my children.

This very special man, now lives in a duplex, has two roommates, cooks, cleans, shops and does laundry for himself. He participates and volunteers with several sports. His father and I and his siblings are so proud of him.

SUMMARY:

DON'T LIE TO ME.

ASK ME.

I AM HERE TO HELP YOU.

WE NEED TO WORK AS A TEAM.

> *Our son has the mind of a child.*
> *Please give him only one direction at a time.*
> *Don't assume he understands what you ask of him.*
> *Ask me how to discipline him. I know what motivates or works to keep him on task.*
> *Incorporate his interests in what you try to teach him. His passion is sports and sharks. (Sadly, no teacher he had ever listened to this advice)*

The last word: Unless you have raised a special needs child you really don't have a clue! But if you LISTEN to the parents who are raising them, your job will be so much easier. Parents are willing to be there and help you every step of the way. JUST ASK, DON'T LIE TO THEM: PLEASE

<u>My final thoughts around Brian.</u> This young man is my nephew. His school story is a sad one and where the education system seriously failed. That is the Situation Reality. There was inclusive education for Brian in his elementary years but NOT in high school where he would, and could have fit into any classroom quite well. I lived very far away and I was able to visit Brian a few times during his high school years. I remember going to the school and seeing 'that room behind the Principal's office.' I thought he didn't belong here. Children with Williams Syndrome are socially

adept, NOT behavior problems.   Brian could have fit in socially IF teachers had allowed it!

And these two parents have assured this young man a good and productive Quality of Life despite his school experience. Brian lives independently quite well. He has traveled to Europe, he is an excellent athlete, and he has spoken confidently about Williams Syndrome to a room full of adults. He continues to amaze me! My sister pointed out the following reference from the Williams Syndrome Fall 2015 online newsletter.

Tomorrow Long Is Too to Wait - Promises Every Special Educator Should Make To Their Students' Parents for Inclusion

1. I promise to stop calling parents who have high expectations and advocate for their children "high maintenance" and I will equally try to discourage the term "high profile" if due process is involved.

2. I promise to presume competence (always assume that your child can learn and is interested in learning) even if they are unable to communicate to me what they know (yet!)

3. I promise to never use the "R" word and to speak up against it when I hear it used in private or public.

4. I promise to ask your input on the educational goals for your child BEFORE the IEP meeting and realize that without your collaboration we have no team.

5. I promise to remember that YOU were your child's first teacher and YOU are an expert on your child...not me.

6. I promise to stop using "what is he/she going to get out of this?" or "they're not ready" as an excuse for not including your child in general education.

7. I promise to never assume I know what goes on at your home or blame your child's challenging behavior at school because of your parenting skills.

8. I promise to Always Be Communicating (ABC) with you about your child (especially the positive things).

9. I promise to keep an open mind and realize that what works with one child does not necessarily work with every child.

10. I promise to always have high expectations for your child and never give up on them...or you.

11. I promise to keep telling your child the reasons why I love to be their teacher.

(These were developed by Tim Villegas for Think Inclusive US. This website is worth taking the time to check out. Also Inclusive Education Canada)

There is nothing more to say....These parents have said it all and I hope You, as a teacher, got what they have taught you.

- Aboriginal Children

The Situation is this: Most provinces and districts in Canada put importance on the teaching of Aboriginal children...some more a focus than others. Nonetheless, the First Nations of our land deserve the best because they were here first; Aboriginal Peoples are an integral part of our North American history. I took this topic seriously as part of my Master's Program work. Let me set the stage here....

Did you know...? Aboriginal People.....

-gave Canada its name and many other names of places

-invented lacrosse and hockey

-helped early settlers by sharing their extensive knowledge of hunting, farming and medicine

-used highly developed herbal medicine which is still used today. Over 200 useful drug-yielding plants were discovered by aboriginal peoples

-have a concern for the environment and ecology as part of their traditional aboriginal culture

-developed over one half of all food crops grown today. Over 100 useful plant species were developed including corn, potatoes, tomatoes, pumpkins and peanuts.

-as Status Indians, in Canada, were not allowed off the reserves between 1882 and 1935 unless they showed a pass

-had many sacred rituals and ceremonies banned by law in Canada from 1884 until 1951. Spiritual leaders were often imprisoned. Spiritual ceremony regalia were confiscated and given to museums or sold to collectors.

-were estimated to number over 12 million people, from the Rio Grande, north when the first Europeans came to North America. Through disease, land clearing, warfare and genocide, the population dropped by 90% in the first century of European contact.

Sources: Gibson:N.M., The American Indian, DC Heath and Co, Lexington, MA: 1980

Weatherfornd, J., Indian Givers, Crown Publishers, NY: 1988

This knowledge AND..the Dark Hidden History not mentioned in our text books around how so many generations of kids were taken to Residential Schools

AND that it wasn't until 1972 when the National Indian Brotherhood asserted Native rights to control Native Education! As a child from the 50's, this information was shock reality for me. I started my Masters work realizing that the majority of Aboriginal children today are not taught by Aboriginal teachers…..so what can I do to bridge the gap..hmmmm

SO …in true Aboriginal form, let me tell you my story. Be patient. There is a worthwhile lesson here.

I grew up close to Aboriginal peoples all my life. I lived in the early days of a small, northern coastal town in B.C. and I thought we were aboriginal because my dad had dark hair and brown eyes.

 Dad and I (1953)

School was a melting pot of cultures, namely Aboriginal, Portuguese, Italian and German but as young kids were never thought of ethnicity. We were all the same! We ate game and fish, smoked salmon, caught crab and dug clams. One day in Grade 3, a

lovely Elder in church told me I was a very polite White Girl. I learned then that my dad's parents were English, directly from the tin mines of Cornwall!

Moving to Vancouver in my teens I was close to a few Aboriginal friends and felt at home because they ate wild game and fish like we did. Living in a very large city with multiple cultures around me was the first time I encountered racism.

Then, young and married, I moved to Haida Gwaii with my husband. I felt right at home. As a teacher here, I was impressed when two colleagues took the English vocabulary needed for primary and developed a series of readers for Haida children. (These readers are still precious to my own children!) After eleven years I was moved to a school within the Haida village of Skidegate. All my new and innovative teaching methods along with the new thinking around best practices and brain-based learning didn't work for me here. I felt like I was drowning, not making a difference. Finally, I watched the Haida teachers and the Haida elder as they came into my class twice a week. They were super teachers and commanded respect from all as I learned a bit about their language, singing, stories and culture. I spent time with these women in their office and I learned three very important lessons from them.

Number One: Listen to Us

Most Aboriginal cultures are Oral Histories. Be Quiet and Listen, especially to the wisdom of elders.

Number Two: Watch Us

Most Aboriginal people, learn skills by watching others. I remember a friend telling me that her grandmother showed her how to take fins off salmon. This grandmother made her watch for three years before handing her a knife.

Number Three: Be Visible

Aboriginal peoples are very intuitive and will pick up on visual cues from you and each other. It was good for me to be seen in the village during celebrations, or even shopping at the local store. My presence showed caring.

Hmmmm so as I had a lot of time crossing a little inter-island ferry on the way home every day, I had time to think! I took seriously what I'd learned and what I knew. I put multi-sensory teaching methods into play Big Time here. I put 2 basketball hoops into my classroom (as this was their favourite game!) and through inventive games I taught these children the multiplication tables and spelling.

I also had a smoker outside my class door and a dehydrator. Working with the Haida teacher and an elder, I tried to make learning relevant. I really loved my time at that school. I look back now and say that those years were the greatest personal and professional growth of my life.

Still, entering a Master's Program, I needed to make more of a connection for all. How can we make a bridge

-with children put in square desks, square classrooms, who culturally understand the power of the circle and four directions?

-with children who have an oral culture?

-with children who are learning European history when their own culture goes back thousands of years?

-with Aboriginal children and teachers who are not aboriginal?

I took the time to learn about Aboriginal History in Canada that I did not know.

I took the time to talk to Aboriginal people in my province about best practices and I found a lot of old resource material that had gone missing among provincial curriculum materials.

I learned that the Village Raises the Child. This concept being very different from my idea of family raising but it made sense. Historically speaking, in an oral culture, EVERY aspect of life from stories to survival depended on instructing the child. Everyone, from grandparents, aunts and uncles had a part in helping to raise the child. This focus is important today.

I learned how Culture, that is, traditions, protocol and customs, embrace every part of Aboriginal life. Put the Politics we hear about in the news on a shelf; LOOK at how beautiful the culture is. I was so impressed with the importance of elders and the respect they commanded. I loved the idea of a Matriarchal Society. I loved how the sick or elderly are never left alone. Learning from the land and appreciating what it gives up for human survival, taking only what is needed. I love the Spiritual significance of all living things. I saw Aboriginal Culture as Being Simple to Understand, Beautiful and Very Classy! Well think about how Aboriginal Peoples have survived for thousands of years before First Contact. The Intelligence to know plants, the movement of animals and seasons still impresses me. Look at the illustrations in Hilary Stewart's book, <u>Indian Fishing, Early Methods of the Northwest Coast</u>(Douglas & McIntyre Ltd., June 1994)…or visit Head Smashed in Buffalo Jump in Alberta…..or stand in front of a large totem pole and wonder how they made that without metal tools..to really understand the incredible intelligence of our First Nations.   Think CULTURE!

I spent two years working on this and ended up putting together a handbook of Do's and Don'ts for New Teachers entering the district. I was pretty pleased with myself as I had worked on this consistently consulting my Haida friends. When I first presented it to them (which was during an assessment time for my project) they listened respectfully and then said, "Great work, Sharlene, but what if teachers do not want to do this?" I was shocked to think that teachers would not want to do this, as I assumed everyone would want to build professionally as a teacher. (What Bubble did I live in, eh?) I made revisions, additions and deletions but this question still came up!!

These lovely elders were gently steering my thinking into thoughts of Teachers who may stereo type Aboriginal peoples or…dare I say it…harbor racist thoughts! OMG, I never thought of this because I had such a respect of Aboriginal cultures growing up!

So off I went on this angle and found an old VCR tape entitle Native Stereotyping. This didn't include my thinking….right?

Or so I thought as I sat and watched this video outlying those terrible spaghetti westerns with the Good White Cowboy and the Noble Savage. Also various books, especially romance …ick! Then the video talked about Jeep Cherokee, the Atlanta Braves baseball team, the Washington Reskins Baseball team and children's toys. Things like this that had been around me for a long time and my un-Aboriginal eyes just did not see! No permission from Aboriginal peoples was given to use these names and trademarks. Think about phrases we know as Hold the Fort! or Circle the Wagons! I get it now..I really get it!

These very special elders were trying to tell me that my handbook of knowledge, my Do's and Don'ts would work **IF teachers were willing to have a hard look at themselves and face their own thoughts and experiences around Aboriginal culture.** It is a valuable lesson to have a hard look at oneself and see how you feel about differing cultures from your own. How were you raised?

To summarize…the Valuable Lessons here are

> Listen, Be Quiet
>
> Watch and Learn
>
> Be Visible
>
> Think CULTURE
>
> Face your own personal feelings around Aboriginal Peoples

You will be a better, caring teacher if you seriously think about these things. The following two quotes say it best and put the nail on the head of this chapter.

"It is an established educational principle that developing a positive, self-image in students is important. In a Native community it is even more so....Students have to contend with prejudice, stereotyping and lower standards of living, which affects their self-image. A Non Native teacher can either affirm or offset many of these negative influences."

John Taylor, First Nations Education In Canada: The Circle Unfolds, (1995), UBC Press

"Children need a strong sense of worth. They need to be treated with respect, dignity and kindness. They need to believe in their abilities. Not enough teachers develop this relationship. Teachers need to understand First Nations people. They need to be soft, friendly, open and equal."

Said to me by my Haida friend, Rosa Bell (1998) who established the first Haida Language Culture program the same year I started teaching on Haida Gwaii. She was part of this Master's Program and she died of breast cancer 3 months before we graduated. Rest in peace my friend. Your words of wisdom will not be forgotten.

In thinking about Canada...we are now a melting pot of so many cultures. Ethnicity is all around us. So when it comes to understand children where English is a Second Language..couldn't the same Five Valuable Lessons I learned here apply? I think so.....

- Final Thoughts around The Kids...

As a teacher you have them for 10 months and for 10 months you Can Make a Difference. Be kind and caring. Establish routines. "Good Morning. It's good to see you!" Believe that Every Child can Learn and Every Child has that Right to Learn! Believe in Inclusive Education for all and NOT putting the 'odd kids' in that room together at the end of the hall. You can be their best advocate if you have that KID SENSE I talked about earlier. If you really want to teach, then you will put in the hours and make sure they all can. You can find modified resources for your weaker learners at the same time challenging those who need it.

The Situation can be though, that You will Protect the CONFIDENTIALITY around your students and their homes at the expense of your reputation. Many a young teacher or new administrator has been grounded to a halt by this reality. I found this to be true in small communities more so than the city. Everyone knows everyone and knows everyone's business. ...or so they think they do. (Your Principal, your fellow teachers, the Social Services, Mental Health people, Your School Councilor are your support for times like this.) I have been accused of being inconsistent around discipline while protecting some serious mental health information about a child no one knew about. Facing this criticism in public, I simply said that there was a lot of information around this situation that I need to keep confidential and that if my reputation takes a hit, then so be it. I would protect any child or any family, if need be, in this way too. The End.

CHAPTER Six:

Situation: Too Many Resources....Which One? Where?

Your Tool Box of Tried and True Resource Treasures are what this brief chapter is about.

I had my treasured books that I kept close to me. They were like good friends. Now a days, it may be a favourite PowerPoint presentation, a Ted Talk, a Podcast, a YouTube video, a blog, a website or an app!

Let me share my favourites…

-Star Teachers of Children in Poverty by Martin Haberman (Kappa Delta Pi, June 1995)

> This was my Go-To Book. It is dog-eared, bookmarked and highlighted. It is about what makes Successful Teachers successful in the inner city schools of the US. Practical and helpful. This is worth getting if it is still in print.

-Reclaiming Youth at Risk: Our Hope for the Future by Larry Bentro, Steve Vanbodkem and Martin Brokenleg (Solution Free Press, 1990, revised edition 2002)

-Restitution: Restructuring School Discipline by Diane Chelsom Gossen (1996) and ALL her awesome, inexpensive resource materials (i.e. My Job, Your Job) Web site is www.realrestitution.com GO check this out!

-<u>The Virtues Project</u> by Linda Kavelin Popov (Jalmar Press, 2000)

> The best source of quick lessons on Character Education. Great vocabulary learning and teaching ideas. Check out her book and the website www.virtuesproject.com

-<u>The Rock Solid Foundation</u>   <u>www.rocksolid.bc.ca</u>

> My favourite whole school anti-bullying strategy. Everyone is talking the same language. Combine the WITS program with some good character education and restitution.

-www.daviesandjohnson.com for <u>Modified Teaching Resources</u>, any grade, any subject. Relatively inexpensive, a site out of Vancouver, BC. I used many of their units so kids with learning disabilities could be included.

-<u>The Seven Habits of Highly Effective People</u> by Stephen Covey (Free Press, 1989)

> When I thought about going into administration, a favourite principal, Ms. Taylor, told me to read everything Stephen Covey had written because he was the guru of Leadership. Wow, what a life changer this was. I also bought the CD and listened to it over and over during those inter-island ferry times. Stephen's seven habits are no nonsense, commonsense! I wish I had read this book as a young teacher. It is good for everyone to read, not just leaders and teachers. The two habits that changed me significantly were
>
> -First Seek to Understand and then to be Understood. Yes! This helped me focus on the issue at hand and

not the emotion of a situation. Listening actively and responding with diplomacy. It calmed lots of storms.

-Sharpen the Saw. Yes! Look after yourself first. Start the day with a walk, quiet time, meditation, exercise, yoga…whatever. Because if the rest of your day goes to (*$&^*&%!! ..you did something right for YOU that day. Every day, before going to work, I walked on a treadmill then I had some quiet reading and reflection from The Good Book over coffee. It sure prepped me for the day, every day.

-Hold on to Your Kids: Why Parents Need to Matter More than their Peers, (Vintage Canada, 2004, 2013) by Gordon Nuefeld, PhD & Gabor Mate, MD

A book I found later in my career but a life changer for sure! It helped me to realize, I was right all along about the importance of making positive connections with kids; the KID SENSE I have talked about in this book. It helped me understand as I got older the reason why it is harder to reach some kids…. Kids who are unattached to adults, whose peers are formulating their values. Oh my..

-Miss Rumphuis by Barbara Cooney, (Viking Press, 1982)

My favourite Year End book of all time. I now see so many others but I read this one at the end of each year. A lovely story about a lady who found a way to make the world a beautiful place. She planted lupines. These wild flowers bloomed at the end of June where I lived and I displayed a bouquet of them. After reading it, I handed each student a packet of wild seeds. I told my students that They are my Seeds and to go out and Make the World a Beautiful Place.

-<u>Where the Sidewalk Ends</u>, by Shel Silverstein (Harper Collins Publishers, 1974)

> Crazy funny poetry to read anywhere, any age with kids. This was a dog-eared book in our family camper too and we can still recite our favourites.."Inside everybody's nose there lives a sharp-toothed snail, and if you stick your finger in, he might bite off your nail….." HAHAHAHA

-<u>The Encyclopedia of Immaturity</u> by the Editors of Klutz, Palo Alto, CA, 2007)

This book aligns with Kid Sense thinking and KID 101. If you want to teach kids, then be one, think like one at their level. This book has soooo many fun things to do with kids that are just that …fun! Before I got this book, I had

-my bag of fav wooden toys I mentioned earlier. Even teenage kids loved to take time to figure out how the string connected to top can make it spin, or how to make a buzz with a big button and string.

-a knowledge string tricks. With a ball of string and scissors you can entertain kids for ages on a long bus trip. You can Google a couple of good books on this out there.

-a knowledge of origami. Fun to do at any age. Make boats, wax crayon the bottom, borrow the water play table from the K room and see how many pennies your boat will take before it sinks.. Or fold paper planes. Stand on the gym stage and see whose plane will fly the farthest. I also learned to make paper origami balloons, cranes, frogs, hats and fish….(FYI, All of these are great too if you need to entertain a toddler in a restaurant. Use the paper placemats.)

-a knowledge of skipping games. If you get a long piece of good braided boat rope (not the yellow plastic stuff), you can do whole class skipping anytime as a wind down or a 12 minute break outside. It's good for any age too!

There are so many awesome resources out there. I loved scouring the tables and conferences for the latest books and thinking. You will find your favourites for sure and then BE SURE to share them! I loved teacher book clubs; they serve good chat and good wine.

CHAPTER Seven:

Situation: Do You Really Want to do this Now?

Each child you meet has a Story and each child you meet has a History.

As a Teacher, you are an Advocate for Children because you are on the Front Line every day. You can report any Situation you think needs looking into…whether it is a disclosure of abuse or sparking a student interest. As a Principal, you become more of an Advocate for Children. I loved this part of the job. I was able to help move troubled kids to a safer home environment, help families cope and find the help they needed…but also help the Teacher and Support Staff with their needs for kids. Too many examples to mention here, but one example I like to remember, was a child who LOVED trains. We made sure he was able to have a short ride on the CPR Holiday Train when it came through our town. He is now on the honor roll in high school. Another example was when a troubled intermediate student wrote a class assignment about wanting a bike park in our town. I took this suggestion to our local Rotary Club. They built one and this young man was informed of the plans and invited to the Grand Opening. As a Superintendent, you can really move and shake the world for kids. My sister said it best when she walked into the Superintendent's office asking for inclusion for Kindergarten for her son, Brian with Williams Syndrome. She said, "He put me on the Superintendent's Advisory Committee for Special Education. I did two years of that before we moved." Enough Said!

As a parting shot, here is my Situation forty years ago and why I became a teacher.......

I disappointed my father when I decided to go into Education.

Being a 1950's man with a Degree in Commerce; a man who worked in HR and PR in the BC lumber & pulp industry 50 weeks out of 52. He took his annual 2 week vacation and away we went to visit the grandparents, aunts, uncles and country cousins. I was the first of his 3 children to leave the nest, so why did I give up a Real Career to go into Education, he wondered.

I was lucky to have wonderful teachers most of my life...

One exception, however, was in Grade 8. I had just moved from the Small Northern Town to the Big City in the south. What a hick I was riding my geeky bicycle to school in a dress. I loved to write stories and poetry and I was pleased with a descriptive paragraph I had written. My teacher was not happy. She took me aside to ask me if I had ever been taught the rudiments of writing. This little one to one interview haunted me all of my life, every time I had to write anything; resumes, report cards, letters, emails, essays, speeches ...and never in my early life did I think I would one day earn a Master's Degree in Education, become a teacher, an administrator, a speaker .....or ever think of writing a book. Amazing, eh?? Later in the year I was able to impress this teacher with my efforts in drama, acting out a scene from a book of one act plays. That was easy for me; being a clown came naturally.

I initially fell in love with Geography thanks to, Mr. Bacon, a wonderful teacher in Grade 9 who made this subject come alive. I remember this robust teacher with an English accent sitting on a desk, pretending he was an Arab relaxing outside his tent in the middle of the desert reading the newspaper. Suddenly he heard the sound of rushing water and he flew off the desk and rolled across the floor. Apparently he had pitched his tent in a waddy, a depression in the desert that is susceptible to flashing flooding. To this day I will never forget what a waddy is….

So it was, that I started taking every Geography course I could find in college thinking it would be fun to be a town planner or a surveyor. Short lived however… I met my husband, who had dreams of becoming a helicopter pilot, which meant both of us would be apart a lot.

About this time I was teaching Sunday School and I really enjoyed preparing for the next lesson. I tried to make the common Bible stories come alive. We used puppetry and role play. Lots of fun. Then the hardest lesson of all; the Easter Story, which to most skeptics is just too weird to believe. I was able to get a copy of the picture book from the movie <u>King of Kings</u> *(Metro-Goldwyn-Mayer, Samuel Bronston Production, U.S.A., 1961.)* I enjoyed reading it to my class showing them the pictures. When I finished, my little charges were enthralled, each believing that I had truly captured the real historical pictures of that time. Oh No! It was a movie..but.. but the story really happened but..um..the pictures were from a movie made about Easter. I don't know if they ever got that and it worried me.

 This got me to thinking about how vulnerable the minds of children really are and I hoped the education system accounted for that. I kept thinking how easy it was to tell kids anything and they would believe me… scary. The curriculum better be doing a good job and our teachers delivering it right!

So..that is why I went into Education! I loved it right away and felt like all new teachers, that I was off to change the world.

As mentioned at the preface, I would hope that the situations in this book jumpstart conversations among educators; some saying, " Yes, I know what she means here. I have had similar experiences and I have another helpful suggestion to share..." Well, DO just that! Share it with others! That is how we become good teachers.

I never looked back and that is the situation!

If you have ploughed through a big chunk of this book, then you have come face to face with many Situations around the Reality of Teaching.

Such responsibility, such pressure.....along with times of laughter and times of tears. Keep that Brag File. I mentioned this earlier. It is all the wonderful things you learn and experience in your career. I kept wonderful notes and pictures from appreciative parents, kids and colleagues.

A good friend still appreciates how I was able to debug math for her daughter in Grade 5. That daughter is now becoming a teacher and the reason I need to finish this book.

Go, Shawna, Go.. My daughter from Another Mother!

You have what it takes to be a Gift to Children. Your Brag File will help you cope during those Down Days. By skimming through it, you will realize the difference you made in the lives of young people. You can put your Head Up and Move On from those difficult days and continue to change lives…one at a time.

AND, my final thought is this: For those of you who think the Situations around Education mentioned in this book are too brash, too real, too honest, too scary and just toooooo Crazy…

Well, you Don't want to Teach Bad Enough!

33189668R00070

Made in the USA
San Bernardino, CA
26 April 2016